Journey to Become

Deep listening leads to a greater self-awareness, invitation to surrender and trust, and intimacy with God

Christine Labrum

ISBN: 1492880647
ISBN - 13: 978-1492880646

Edited by Dana Ergenbright
Layout and design by Heather Westbrook (www.hwdesigns.info)

Thoughts on *Journey to Become*

"Christine's tender words and beautiful drawings will immediately draw you into her journey of reflection and listening for God, and her thought-provoking questions and Scripture will encourage you to embark on your own journey towards gaining a fresh perspective of yourself and your God."

-Judy Hartzel, Bible teacher and mentor

"Christine has invited us to listen on so many levels—to Scripture, to the Spirit of Christ, and to our own hearts, minds, senses and souls. By telling, drawing, and painting her own story, she shows courage, vulnerability, discovery, possibility, and the gifts of darkness and Light in black, brilliant white, and living color. Space opens before us and within us. May we move into the space to listen to the often-missed reality of a God who is the living Word, drawing us ever closer to His heart to heal our wounds and transform us into the likeness of His beloved Son."

-Doreen Miller, MD and spiritual director

"*Journey to Become* is a wonderfully unique book. The author's verbal and visual skill fit seamlessly together inviting the reader to look over the shoulder of a woman as she honestly and passionately pursues God."

-Bryan Maier, PsyD, associate professor, counseling and psychology, Biblical Seminary

"Christine has opened up her heart to the world-at-large in this interactive book to share her own journey to become, so that we may receive that invitation into communion with God. Through poetry, art, quotes, Scripture, her own journal entries and space for our own journaling we are given the time and the space—IF we can but choose—to enter into the silence...the stillness...and LISTEN for God's voice. Feel the freedom to allow your own soul some time and space to rest...and to listen...and to become. I know a great starting point: *Journey to Become*!"

-Maggie Robbins, spiritual director and author of *Enjoy the Silence*

"I often describe the act of creating (and offering others the space to create) as a slip-n-slide to the throne; it's the easiest, most fun (and messy!) way of finding myself connected to God. And as I read, reflected on, and continue to invite the God of Christine's journey to be near me as well, I find myself on the slippiest of slides and wanting to invite all my friends along for the ride."

-Aletheia Schmidt, artist and spiritual director

"It is a rare gift when someone chooses courage and shares their story for the good of others. In *Journey to Become*, Christine lays bare her heart while inviting us, the readers, to discover our own journey deeper into God's heart. Chris's artwork is as beautiful as her story and when coupled with questions only Chrisy can ask, they challenge us to listen for God in a whole new way. I will read this book over and over and, I suspect, grow closer to God each time."

-Beth Speed, wife, mother, and friend

"My heart was immediately drawn to abide in Jesus more deeply as I pondered the pictures, lingered on the stories, and considered the tender questions in each chapter for my own heart. Christine's book *Journey to Become* has helped me to uncover parts of my heart landscape that I didn't even know existed...and it has lead to sweet freedom in my journey and a deeper intimacy with God."

-Heather Bickel Stevenson, RN and spiritual director

"When Christine joined our small group, we unknowingly had the privilege of experiencing this book while in its development. Often Christine would show us her most recent drawing, sharing the scripture and spiritual journey behind the created piece. As God stirred, we each had our own unique response. Likewise, in *Journey to Become*, Christine guides the reader gently and thoughtfully closer to the heart of God."

-Margie Orehowsky and Judy Goehler, friends on the journey

In Gratitude

O my strength, I will sing praises to You; for God is my stronghold, the God who shows me lovingkindness. Psalm 59:17 NASB

Abba Father, Lord Jesus, Spirit of God, I thank You for Your love and Your life. You have captured my heart all over again.

Mark, thank you for your love and loyalty—they have been a haven and a resting place. Thank you for supporting me in this project and lending your skills as needed. Your belief in me has given me courage to embrace the journey to become all God intended me to be, and I am grateful. I love you.

Hannah, my dragon girl, I love you. God has given you a passion for life, a heart that cares deeply for others, and a willingness to serve. Michaella, my little lady hawk, I love you. God has given you an innate strength, clarity of mind, and a creative, imaginative heart. My daughters, it is my joy to be your mama, and I am thankful for you.

Mom and Dad, I will forever be grateful for the foundation of faith you provided for me. Our family was built upon the belief that God is and that He is good. As a child you taught me of my need of God for salvation and for life, and your love provided a greenhouse for me to respond to God. Thank you.

Preston Gillham, you have been a guide and a friend on the spiritual journey and the creative journey. Your insight, authenticity, kindness, and thought-provoking questions have caused me to journey deeper into the heart of God and to more fully be who God created me to be. Thank you.

The Prayer Team
I am thankful for the men and women who partnered with me in prayer as I completed this book project.

Debbie Fareno, you have been a spiritual friend for a long time, and so often our lives have paralleled along the way. Thank you for believing in me and sharing the journey. Beth Speed, you have listened to my reflections for over 20 years, and it has been a joy to connect over this project. Thank you for your careful reading of each section—you offered thoughtful suggestions and insight. Margie Orehowsky, Judy Goehler, and

Joan Miller, I am grateful for your companionship over the last four years. Our small group has been a safe place to listen for God together. Deb Churchill, Pam and Ken Wohltmann, Heather Stevenson, Jane Seitz, Jocelyn and Sean Flenders, Connie Lezenby, Judy Hartzel, Betsy Smith, and Pastor Kent Berghuis, each of you have blessed me in this endeavor.

Kairos
And I am grateful for Kairos: School of Spiritual Formation, for the space they offer for being attentive to God. The gifts I have received from the Visualizing Your Spiritual Journey retreats, the Spiritual Direction Training program, and the Kairos community have made an eternal difference in my life. Marcus Pomeroy, Peg Greiner, and Cheryl Lehman, thank you for leading and teaching, and providing a safe place for us to "become." Thank you.

Heather Westbrook, designer, and Dana Ergenbright, editor, I could not have done this without you. Thank you.

In Memory

This book is dedicated to:

Daniel Smith

Brother of mine, as kids we built Lego creations side by side, and as adults we built our lives. Some of the pieces you built with were strong and uniquely shaped, some were challenging to discern how they fit, and some got broken along the way. I saw God in you, and with joy, I remember your gifts and your strengths. I am grateful for your love for my girls; you were a fabulous uncle. And I am grateful for your friendship. Your name means "God is my judge," and I envision you standing before God, experiencing His love and grace more fully than you ever could have imagined here. I love you, and I miss you.

Michelle Maier

Sister of my heart, God brought us together for a season. We shared a heart for mothering and ministry and a love of beauty. You were one of the most self-aware and perceptive individuals I have known, and I learned from you. Our conversations, often over coffee, always stirred something deep in me, and I came away longing for more of God and grateful for the gift of a kindred spirit. Despite your battle with cancer, you companioned me through some of the most difficult and significant years of my life. I love you, and I miss you.

An Invitation to Listen

This book is an invitation to slow down and listen deeply for God, the One who loves you most.

As I share my journey into deeper listening, consider your own walk with God. There is space to journal, and I encourage you to write the things that echo softly or shout loudly within you as you reflect on your own story. Write the questions that surface, feel the emotions that stir, and offer them to God. Listen for all that He will say, not just here, but in all the corners of your life.

I heard God's invitation to listen through His gentle whispers and subtle nudges. In my external world, crisis, grief, and a sense of isolation left me aching to hear from God. I faced choices where I longed for discernment and God's leading. I needed to create space in my life to listen, often in silence, and it has made all the difference. The gifts have been a greater self-awareness, invitation to surrender and trust, and deeper intimacy with God.

What would it look like to create space to listen more deeply for the voice of God? Would it involve turning things off, letting go, stepping out, being still, turning toward hope, looking back, embracing courage, simplifying, repenting, or something else? For me, it has been all of those choices, and more.

Our spiritual practices enable us to be attentive and to open our hearts and minds to God. Our practices include prayer, studying Scripture, serving others, and much more. But the practices that invite us to slow down, be still, and be quiet can get lost in a culture that values productivity and activity. This slowing down, however, is vital to our well-being. In the stillness we can listen for God.

My drawings and the thoughts I share in this book come from my conversations with God, time spent in the Scriptures, and time in community. I want to share enough of my story to offer a context for the artwork and reflections. But my hope is that the Scriptures, the questions, and the images will be a unique avenue for listening to God's voice to you.

There is a reflection written for each drawing. You may want to skip that and spend time with the drawing, the questions, and the Scripture first. Consider what would most deeply invite you into communion with God. May God gently bless you as you listen for Him.

— Christine

Table of Contents

My soul longs for You, as a parched land.
Teach me the way in which I should walk;
For to You I lift up my soul.

Psalm 143:6b, 8b NASB

Longing for Something More

A Whispered Invitation

Early in 2009 I had a sense that something was going to shift in my life in the coming years, but I was uncertain what this transition would look like. I heard God's invitation to pay attention and to listen.

I was coordinator of the MOPS (Mothers of Preschoolers) group at my church, and as a stay-at-home mom with two preschoolers, my life was full. There was a desire stirring within me that I could not name, a yearning for something. Have you ever felt that niggling feeling within that seems to be asking for your attention? Perhaps I could have described it as a desire for more of God. Although I could not define it, I knew that God was at the center of it. My caterpillar existence, with a low-lying perspective and a gnawing hunger, was about to grow very dark for a while as I entered a chrysalis sort of season. But that would not be the end of the story.

I had walked with God for as long as I could remember. I had experienced Jesus as my Savior at a young age and then as my Companion and Teacher. In later years I experienced the intimacy of God as my Father, Abba, and in recent years the Holy Spirit had been my counselor, the God within. At 38 years old, I had learned thus far to turn toward God, whatever the crisis or whatever the question. There had been ups, downs, and plateaus in my journey, but the road was about to take a sharp turn. The coming season would hold depletion, challenge, and grief, but there would also be joy, fullness, and life. And I would never be the same.

In recent years, more often than not, I felt weary, fragmented, and frazzled. Tears came easily whenever I stopped to be still. I struggled with fatigue and recurring headaches. The sense of feeling overwhelmed would become very heavy every few months, so my husband, Mark, would take the reins for an afternoon or an overnight and watch the girls. I would retreat. I would lean in hard to God, refill my diminishing resources, and I would press on. Isn't that what we are supposed to do?

I believed deeply in the MOPS ministry that I coordinated, and I was passionate about leading well, but I was so weary. At this time my closest mom friend was fighting stage 4 breast cancer, and my brother battled addiction. My husband's job was demanding, so I often felt like I was parenting alone in the day-to-day challenges. Motherhood is a gracious gift, and I treasured our little girls, but I found the demands of mothering preschoolers to be a difficult fit for my reflective personality. Our lives hold burdens, challenges, and losses. These were mine at this time.

As I was attentive I started to see the opportunities God brought my way. After attending a workshop on wholeness, led by Yvonne (an MDiv student interning at our church and a psychologist by profession), I started meeting with her. She compassionately listened to my story and my weariness. The first day I sat with her she said to me, "I think you would benefit from a spiritual director." I did not even know what a spiritual director was, but tears filled my eyes and something stirred within me.

Because of Yvonne's encouragement and our conversations, I sought counseling for healing of old wounds. God led me to a counselor who was also a spiritual director. This was a valuable step in moving forward. The investment of time, resources, and spiritual and emotional energy to bring healing and closure to old wounds prepared me for all that was coming.

A New Calling

It had been a normal spring day, but I can envision the moment. I was driving, running errands locally, and a thought startled me. *I want to be a spiritual director.* It was an uninvited desire that strutted into my awareness without warning. Those who know me don't expect me to be decisive, and I wrestled with this sense of calling in later months, but on that day, in my gut, I knew that spiritual direction was what I was to do.

Did God plant that desire in me or whisper a calling? There had been no word in my vocabulary for this ministry of companionship until these recent months. But despite a sketchy definition of spiritual direction, a spark had been lit in my soul. I was drawn to this way of supporting and being with others as they sought God and listened for His voice. I started reading and researching this ancient role of companioning another in their walk with God. Energy and joy sparkled within me for the first time in a long time.

I began praying and pursuing possible avenues for training. I was drawn to the spiritual direction training program offered at Kairos: School of Spiritual Formation that would begin in the fall. I noticed the intensity and impatience in me. But one afternoon as I sat outside and watched a storm approach, God clearly told me to wait. I was disappointed, but I realized my soul was not ready. I needed stillness and rest, and I did not know what the coming year would hold. But God did.

It was weeks after this directive to wait for His timing that God began to reveal to me that some of the ways I managed life were more self-filled than grace-filled. Thus, despite a deep desire for God and a desire to minister, my lack of self-knowledge had allowed me to become depleted.

Depletion

So, in July 2009, as I allowed myself to hear His revelation, I experienced the depths of my depletion and desperation—and I crashed. As I met with my counselor, she was there to say, "Be where you are."

This time I did not pull myself up by my bootstraps and return to business as usual after a short break. This time I stopped trying to manage everything. I felt like a failure, and the hazy hope of recent months threatened to dissipate. I pleaded with God for guidance, and I heard God ask me to let go of the MOPS ministry and pass the baton. So I did. My friend, Michelle, called me "courageous"—I felt like far less.

I noticed the emotions that surfaced, and I allowed myself to feel those emotions. They were messages from within, and I listened as God interpreted. I was attentive to the fatigue in my body, and it grew heavier. I learned how to receive help and ask for help in those summer months, a lesson in humility. I knew that many would not understand this intangible wilderness I had entered; I wasn't sure that I did. My withdrawal from ministry, my slowing down and looking inward, could appear very self-absorbed. Although I worried about how people perceived me, I needed to let go of any effort to manage that as well. I sensed God's invitation to be wholly honest.

So I stopped, and I listened deeply. This time I waited on the Lord, not simply for relief and just enough grace to go on, but I waited to hear all that He would say. I felt desperate in my need of God, not even sure that I could say that I loved Him because my neediness felt so great. God provided a few encouraging voices to affirm the path He was leading me down, and they were a lifeline, but they were few. Little did I realize that this was only the beginning of hope, a deep abiding hope, not only in God but also in what He was doing in me, and what He would eventually do through me.

At this time I had a small spiral sketchbook. In these first weeks I was too foggy to analyze and too uncertain to journal anything of significance. But I did jot down phrases or words, verses, quotes, and sketches of my experience of myself and of God. It was the seed of this book.

I have walked with God for many years. I have a solid theology of God and a love for the Scriptures. But these recent years have been a gift. I have learned to be more still, to embrace silence, to be more truthful, and to listen more deeply. Sometimes God speaks, and sometimes He is silent, but the listening has made all the difference.

God has revealed to me more of myself. I have known for a long time that He knows me better than I do; now I know more of myself than I did. Blind spots are dangerous, and I am more aware of how to discern where mine are. I have heard God's invitation to surrender, and I have experienced Him as trustworthy in the surrendering. I have fallen in love with God all over again, and the intimacy is a treasure. These are my reflections on the journey into deep listening that leads us to a deeper self-awareness, an opportunity to surrender, and a deeper intimacy with God.

Invitation

Weary heart, deep emptiness,
fragmented and frazzled,
I can't keep the pace.

Energy and passion a distant memory,
I've lost the joy of the dance,
Celebration has ceased.

Striving, performing, trying so hard.
Empty...so very, very empty.
Dreadfully inadequate and longing for escape.

An invitation whispered,
a moment of choice,
honesty requested.
Truth has asked to dance with me.

Hesitation, and a surge of fear,
Yet, desperation presses me towards Him.
I tremble with longing for something I lack.

Music starts and emotions surge,
Uncertainty cloaks my soul but I relinquish control.
Pretense steps back and Truth takes my hand.

Shamefully awkward, I can't find the rhythm.
I am clumsy; the tension is real.
Glancing at watching eyes, my face flushes with shame.

He lifts my chin and His eyes draw mine,
I see His heart and mine is set free.
I stumble and His arms hold my weight.
I lean into His presence, Truth leads me.

Just to be. I'm not sure that I can.
Just to be. And to rest in His arms.
Just to be. And to follow His lead.

Created for this dance, I was created for this dance.
Truth is my partner and He leads.

I dance with Truth. I dance my song. I dance my dance.
Freedom fills my heart, passion moves my spirit.
My soul has wings, beauty is birthed and life breathes.

christine

Journey to Become

What is God's vision for you? He created you with design and purpose, and He will complete what He has begun. What is God doing in your life now?

I had an appointment with my counselor one Thursday afternoon in July of 2009. As I sat to journal before I met with her, I could feel my overwhelming exhaustion. It wasn't just my body that was tired; my soul was weary. I wanted the world to stop, and I wanted to cry for a very long time. This was the beginning of a dark season in my life, but it was not without hope.

That weekend I retreated. As I sat in a hotel, alone with God, the words from a chorus we sang at church ran through my conscious thoughts: "Strength will rise as we wait upon the Lord, wait upon the Lord." I needed to wait upon the Lord. In time, fatigue would become strength and light would fill my world again. But there was some 'waiting' to be done first.

That summer of depletion was when the image of the butterfly first started to flutter in my soul. I could hear God's whisper that transformation often occurs when all is dark and hidden. I was quite aware that hope is to be found in one place, or one person rather. God is the source of our hope, and I was being invited to listen more deeply to Him.

Thus one evening I combined the images of a butterfly and a face to create *Becoming*. God does not waste those places of darkness, wilderness, or suffering. The darkness of the chrysalis would not be forever. My friend Michelle sent me a card that said, "Caterpillars really do become butterflies." How kind of God to place that creature in the world to remind us that transformation is possible. This drawing was about hope and vision.

He who began a good work in you will carry it on to completion until the day of Christ Jesus.

Philippians 1:6b

But whenever someone turns to the Lord, the veil is taken away.

For the Lord is the Spirit, and wherever the Spirit of the Lord is, there is freedom.

So all of us who have had that veil removed can see and reflect the glory of the Lord.

And the Lord—who is the Spirit—makes us more and more like him as we are changed into his glorious image.

2 Corinthians 3:16-18

We pursue God because, and only because, he has first put an urge within that spurs us to pursuit. "No man can come to me," said our Lord, "Except the Father which hath sent me draw him." And it is by that prevenient drawing that God takes from us every vestige of credit for the act of coming. The impulse to pursue God originates with God, but the outworking of that impulse is following hard after Him.

A.W. Tozer, *The Pursuit of God*

15

Becoming, 2009

What will
happen if
I stop and
listen to God's
invitation?

• • • • • •

Will I accept
His invitation
to wander
the corridors
of my heart?

• • • • • •

Will I respond
to His call
to rest,
repentance,
and renewal?

• • • • • •

Will I yield to
His healing
touch? Will I
listen? Will I
trust?

• • • • • •

Will I allow
Him to lead
me into
freedom and
fruitfulness?

Invitation to Depart

This drawing came about after spending time in Isaiah 42:16-17 with my small group, using the practice of lectio divina. Lectio is an ancient practice of reading Scripture with an open heart and attentiveness to the Spirit. The passage is read four times with a few minutes of silence between each reading. Many of the drawings created after 2012 came out of time spent listening for God with Scripture through this ancient practice.

As we journey we encounter many doors. Each one offers a choice; we face a decision to go through it or not. It is often an invitation to journey somewhere else.

Much is unknown beyond this door. One must leave what is familiar to embrace the new. An invitation to something new can be daunting, and there is risk in leaving what is known. Darkness and a cold, familiar security exist within the high stone walls of this place. How long have we been in this place? Why did we initially stop here? What do I truly desire?

Has God placed a door before you? What has He revealed to you of the place where you are? Has He whispered an invitation to you in the deep and quiet places in your heart?

This door has a small stained glass window that hints at light on the other side, and the image reveals a path beyond the door. The rocks have been cleared away from the beginning of the path, but there is much ground yet to travel. There could be segments of ease or of hardship and challenge on the path ahead. But it is dawn, and the light is growing brighter. There is adventure ahead.

*I have put before you an
open door...*

Revelation 3:8 NASB

*I will lead the blind by ways they have not known,
along unfamiliar paths I will guide them;
I will turn the darkness into light before them and make the rough places smooth.*

*These are the things I will do; I will not forsake them.
But those who trust in idols, who say to images, 'You are our gods,'
will be turned back in utter shame.*

Isaiah 42:16-17

The Doorway, 2012

_____

_____

_____

_____

_____

_____

_____

_____

_____

_____

_____

_____

_____

_____

Has God placed a door before me?

• • • • • •

What has He revealed to me of the place where I am?

• • • • • •

Has He whispered an invitation to me in the deep and quiet places in my heart?

Held Secure

When God invites you to journey into the unknown, it is the promise and the experience of being deeply loved that provides the courage to join Him.

In 2004 I began a series of drawings shortly after the birth of my first daughter, Hannah Grace. Although creativity had always played a role in my life, it had been a long time since I had done any significant work. In an effort to process this major life transition of becoming a mother, I sat with a photo of my daughter and me, and I started to draw. In time I completed a series. And then after the birth of my second daughter, Michaella Joy, I added to the collection.

This pen and ink drawing, *Cherished*, was one of the final pieces done in these early years of motherhood. This drawing of Michaella was created from a photo taken by my sister, Cathy, a week after Michaella's birth.

I love this drawing because there is an element of metaphor in the image. There is a strong sense of being cherished and protected. The care of a mother for her child is a shadow of God's intimate care for us and commitment to us. God tenderly holds us with a love that takes a lifetime to begin to comprehend. I continue to learn about God and His love for me. And I learn how to offer my love to Him, despite how childish and needy it often is.

An identity grounded in God would mean that when we think of who we are, the first thing that would come to mind is our status as someone who is deeply loved by God.

David Benner, *The Gift of Being Yourself*

Held Secure

"The Lord your God is with you,
he is mighty to save.
He will take great delight in you,
he will quiet you with His love,
he will rejoice over you with singing."

Zephaniah 3:17 NIV 1984

Cherished, 2007

Am I aware of the depths of God's love for me?

• • • • • •

How can I turn toward God and lean into His love?

• • • • • •

If I am loved and He is good, can I trust His invitation?

Held Secure

Noticing on the Journey

Something happens when I pause to be fully present, to be where I am. What happens when I notice what surrounds me and what is within me?

In this drawing, I am holding my daughter Hannah on the beach and her eyes are fixed on the ocean waves. I am reminded to notice. What happens within me as I stand at the ocean's edge and pause to notice the waves as they lap the sandy shore? What wonder stirs in my heart as I ponder the endless expanse of the sea? How do my thoughts turn to the Creator of this vast, and seemingly endless, horizon?

How many invitations has God whispered to my soul? As I notice the movements within my own heart, do I become more aware of the God who gave me life? Do I recognize the privilege and dignity that God has given to me as I make choices?

As emotions rise within my soul, do I recognize how God has equipped me with internal indicators that speak of the state of my heart and mind? As my body feels strength, feels pain, or feels fatigue, do I realize that I have been equipped to discern my body's capacity and its needs? Do I notice the whispers inside of me or outside of me? Do I listen?

For since the creation of the world His invisible attributes, His eternal power and divine nature, have been clearly seen, being understood through what has been made.

Romans 1:20a NASB

How many are your works, Lord!
In wisdom you made them all;
the earth is full of your creatures.

May the glory of the Lord endure forever;
may the Lord rejoice in his works—
he who looks at the earth, and it trembles,
who touches the mountains, and they smoke.

I will sing to the Lord all my life;
I will sing praise to my God as long as I live.

May my meditation be pleasing to him,
as I rejoice in the Lord.

Psalm 104:24, 31-34

Noticing on the Journey

Hannah Watching the Waves, 2004

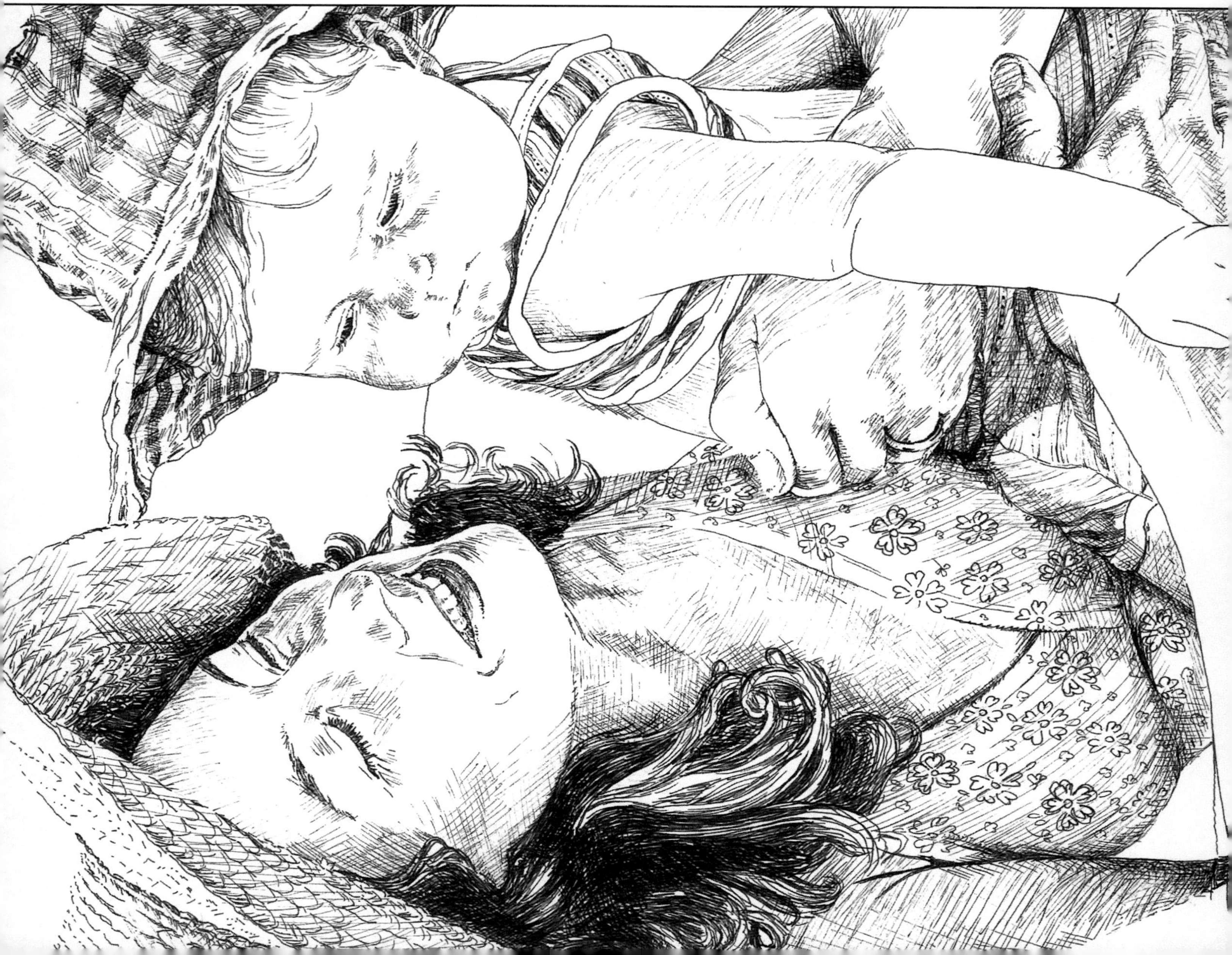

What captures my attention and invites me to notice?

• • • • • •

How do I see God's hand in that which I notice?

Do You See Me?

Sometimes my heart longs to be acknowledged. I want to be seen and to be known. But do I realize that I am known beyond what I could ever dream? God knows me more fully than I know myself, more fully than I will ever know myself. The triune God is my Creator, Redeemer, and Sustainer. Do I realize that He can enable me to see myself with greater clarity and understanding?

I remember one birthday as a young adult, just a couple years after I graduated college. It was the first birthday that I celebrated away from family. And although my family never did things in a huge way, we always remembered and celebrated birthdays. That day on my way to work I remember talking with God and simply asking if He would provide a cake for me for my birthday. Who makes a cake for you besides your mom?

I had not told anyone of my prayer, but that year I received two surprise cakes from different friends. I knew that God had seen me through these gifts in a unique and memorable way. I noticed.

You have searched me, Lord, and you know me.
You know when I sit and when I rise;
you perceive my thoughts from afar.

You discern my going out and my lying down;
you are familiar with all my ways.

Before a word is on my tongue you, Lord, know it completely.
You hem me in behind and before, and you lay your hand upon me.

Such knowledge is too wonderful for me,
too lofty for me to attain...

For you created my inmost being;
you knit me together in my mother's womb.

I praise you because I am fearfully and wonderfully made;
your works are wonderful, I know that full well.

My frame was not hidden from you when I was made in the secret
place, when I was woven together in the depths of the earth.

Your eyes saw my unformed body; all the days ordained for me
were written in your book before one of them came to be.

Psalm 139:1-6, 13-16 NIV 1984

Love Sees Me, 2004

Have I felt invisible? Do I long to be seen and truly known?

. . . . . .

When have I experienced myself as known by God?

. . . . . .

What stirs in my heart at the thought that God sees me and loves me with a love beyond definition?

Invitation to Rest

Why is it so difficult to rest? We live in a culture addicted to busyness and productivity. Space to be still and time to rest are not valued. And yet God designed us to need rest.

God created the world in six days, and then He chose to rest on the seventh day. Startling if one thinks about it. He is God after all and not bound by time or limited resources.

And then God gave us a command to honor the Sabbath when He gave the Ten Commandments to Moses. He directed us to set apart a day to honor Him and to rest from our work. What kindness!

We are created to work and to rest. It is an act of trust and dependence to set aside time for Sabbath. It reminds us that we have limits.

I grew up in a family where the rhythm of Sabbath was respected. My dad valued taking one day of the week to do things differently and to be more attentive to God. That value honored God and was a gift to our family. What life rhythm of work and rest is familiar to you?

I continue to learn how to be intentional and guard Sabbath in a way that honors God and benefits our family. I believe Sabbath is not just for leisure and physical rest but also to give us space to enjoy our Creator. Each one needs to discern how to honor God in a way that is good for body, soul, and spirit. In the summer of 2009 I heard God's invitation to rework my life rhythm, including my rhythm for Sabbath.

*Come to Me, all who are weary and
heavy-laden, and I will give you rest.*

*Take My yoke upon you, and learn from Me,
for I am gentle and humble in heart;
and you will find rest for your souls.*

For My yoke is easy and My burden is light.

Matthew 11:28-30 NASB

*This is what the Lord says:
"Stand at the crossroads
and look; ask for the
ancient paths, ask where
the good way is, and walk
in it, and you will find rest
for your souls."*

Jeremiah 6:16a

Dangerous tired is an atmospheric condition of the soul that is volatile and portends the risk of great destruction. It is a chronic inner fatigue accumulating over months and months, and it does not always manifest itself in physical exhaustion. In fact it can be masked by excessive activity and compulsive over working. When we are dangerously tired we feel out of control, compelled to constant activity by inner impulses that we may not be aware of.

Ruth Haley Barton, *Invitation to Solitude and Silence*

Hannah Sleeping, 2004

_____

_____

_____

_____

_____

_____

_____

_____

_____

_____

_____

_____

_____

_____

_____

What is the present condition of my soul and my body?

• • • • • •

Is God inviting me to find rest in Him? How can I trust Him enough to let go?

• • • • • •

How does choosing to Sabbath deepen my relationship with God?

Invitation to Rest

Held in His Hands

My brother Dan died and went home to be with God in August of 2009.

That year I had been attentive to God's nudges and whispers. When summer came I was weary and depleted. I heard God's invitation to rest and to "let go." On August 6th I had fully passed the baton of leadership for MOPS to another capable and godly young woman. On August 7th, the following day, I found out that my brother who was 3 years younger than I had died at 36 years old. God had known what was coming in my life, as He always does.

The day after Dan died my husband and I walked the block and a half from our house to his apartment. Life seemed surreal and I could barely grasp that Dan was gone. A Monarch butterfly flew very close to us and landed nearby in the grass. It had meandered slowly in the air, brilliant in the sunlight. It appeared to be brand new, perhaps trying its wings out for the first time. I placed my hand on the grass close to the butterfly, and with encouragement it moved into my hand. The creature sat very still, cupped in my hand, as we walked back to our house.

My husband, Mark, took its photograph and then I set it down on the flowers in front of my house. After a couple minutes the butterfly slowly took off and it flew upward in large circles. It flew high above the trees, and then flew off into the distance. It was as if God allowed us to see by creative metaphor that all would be well. My brother Dan was finally free, complete in his transformation, and one day our own grief would be transformed into hope too.

The image of a butterfly is powerful. And the butterfly held by gentle hands speaks to me of the God who tenderly holds His children through every transformation. One day our transformation will indeed be complete, as we trust in Him.

Even to your old age I will be the same, and even to your graying years I will bear you!

I have done it, and I will carry you; and I will bear you and I will deliver you.

Isaiah 46:4 NASB

As strange as it may sound, desperation is a really good thing in the spiritual life. Desperation causes us to be open to radical solutions, willing to take all manner of risk in order to find what we are looking for.

Ruth Haley Barton,
Invitation to Solitude and Silence

Held in His Hands

For from days of old they have not heard nor perceived by ear, nor has the eye seen a God besides You, who acts in behalf of the one who waits for Him.

Isaiah 64:4 NASB

Held by Love, 2009

_____

_____

_____

_____

_____

_____

_____

_____

_____

_____

_____

_____

_____

_____

_____

When have
I felt fragile
and alone?

••••••

When have I
experienced
God's hands
holding me?

••••••

Is it possible
to be held
securely
and not
know it?

Holding in His Hands

Paths Beyond the Mess

There are so many times when emotions run high and thoughts get tumbled in the raging torrent.

This was one of those days when my internal landscape was encountering stormy weather. My tangled emotions and racing thoughts seemed to define my reality, so I sat down to attempt to put them on paper. I needed to own the emotions that were mine and offer them to God. Through this visual prayer I hoped to surrender and listen to Father's voice.

I started to play with colors and marks on the paper to visualize the internal mess. At first there was chaos on the page with heavy dark colors, stark on the white background, reflecting lingering grief. Intense colors and abrupt marks spoke of conflict and woundedness. But I continued.

And as I placed my paintbrush to the paper, I found myself creating some shades and marks that reflected movement that was intentional, even hopeful. Over the course of a day or so, I started to see paths of grace that moved upward and beyond the tangled mess where I began.

As I prayerfully reflected, I could name the paths of grace. Internally, I had placed conflict and chaos in God's hands while I placed paint on the paper. In the process I had surrendered the mess and God had settled my heart. The shift in my heart became evident in my drawing. And at the center of my tangle, there was a swirl of energy and beauty that spoke of the rich gift of relationship that I had been blessed to receive, although the shadow of grief was yet a part of the image. This drawing was my prayer.

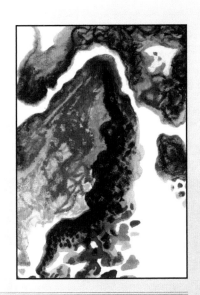

Therefore, as God's chosen people, holy and dearly loved, clothe yourselves with compassion, kindness, humility, gentleness and patience.

Bear with each other and forgive one another if any of you has a grievance against someone.

Forgive as the Lord forgave you. And over all these virtues put on love, which binds them all together in perfect unity.

Let the peace of Christ rule in your hearts, since as members of one body you were called to peace.

And be thankful.

Colossians 3:12-15

Paths Beyond the Mess

There are desires at work within us that work against the life of the Spirit within us—desires rooted in selfish ambition, pride, lust, fear, self-protection and many other unexamined motives. These desires lurk within all of us, and that is why giving any attention at all to desire feels like opening Pandora's box. But it is even riskier to refuse to acknowledge what's real within us, because whether we acknowledge them or not, these dynamics are at work wielding a subterranean power over us. Their power only gets stronger the longer we repress them. How much safer it is for ourselves and everyone around us if we open up our desires in Jesus' presence and allow him to help us sift through them.

Ruth Haley Barton, *Sacred Rhythms*

Is there a knot in my stomach, a tangle in my emotions, and a tension in a relationship?

• • • • • •

Is God inviting me to a path that leads beyond the conflict?

• • • • • •

What do honesty and love look like here in the messiness?

Paths Beyond the Mess

Invitation to Repent

This butterfly was photographed by my sister, Cathy, but I took many liberties with the drawing. The meaning, for me, is somewhat hidden in the image.

This was a time when God was revealing my struggle with the real and perceived expectations of others and my own drive and attachment to seeking approval from others. God gently drew me to repentance.

Imagine a butterfly with a string tied to its wing, held back from the freedom it was intended to have. When I tie myself to the expectations of others, seeking their approval above God's, I have abdicated the freedom I have in Christ. It is my responsibility to steward the trust of my life well, not to abdicate it to another.

This butterfly has a small piece torn out of its wing. It is as if the creature has pulled free from a string tied to its fragile wing. I am reminded that there are consequences to trying to please others for the wrong reasons. A friend once challenged me that compliance is not a positive character quality. Love is sacrificial but not due to fear or pride.

I am grateful for God's kindness that leads us to repentance. Although this butterfly had a small tear in its wing, it is not tied to anything. There is growth in this area of my life, and consequently this image is filled with brilliant color and energy.

Is God's kindness inviting you to repent? What are the strings that attach you to the ground, like a kite held by a human hand? Will "letting go" release you to fly unhindered wherever God leads you to go? Repentance, although humbling to be certain, draws us close to the heart of God, freeing us to be who He intended us to be.

Self-knowledge is God's gift, not the result of your introspection.... There is no substitute for meeting God in your depths if you really desire this knowing. Praying that you might see yourself as God sees you takes courage. But if done with the deep assurance that the self you seek to know is already known and deeply loved by God, it is absolutely possible.

David Benner, *The Gift of Being Yourself*

Search me, God, and know my anxious heart;

test me, and know my anxious thoughts,

see if there is any offensive way in me, and lead me in the way everlasting.

Psalm 139:23-24

Freedom, 2010

Is God's kindness inviting me to repentance and to deeper freedom?

· · · · · ·

Have I tied my fragile wing to something that God never intended, to something that holds me hostage?

Even the darkness is not dark to You,
and the night is as bright as the day.
Darkness and light are alike to You.

Psalm 139:12 NASB

The Darkness Deepens

The Next Day

The coming year would not be an easy one. The summer of 2009 had been a time to face my depletion, slow down, and reevaluate. We intentionally made some changes at home to slow the pace, and by the August 6th MOPS leadership team meeting I had completely handed over my responsibilities to the team and the new coordinator.

I chose to withdraw from the MOPS community to give the new coordinator space to embrace her position. This was a difficult decision, but I was confident that it was appropriate and it was what God asked of me. Although relinquishing my role in MOPS relieved me of many responsibilities, I would miss the community and the relationships.

The next day, August 7th, the phone rang. It was my mom calling to tell me that my dad was on his way to pick up a spare key I kept for my brother's apartment a block and a half away. Dan's boss had called my parents, concerned because he had not been to work for a couple days and he was not answering his phone. My parents were aware Dan had been struggling with addiction again, so it was not a call they took lightly. Although the girls and I had been at Dan's apartment a few days earlier, enjoying a movie and ice cream, I was uneasy about what my dad would find at the apartment.

That afternoon my friend Michelle stopped by to look at a dresser I was giving away. I was so grateful to see her drive up to my house. I shared my anxious heart and the happenings of the afternoon. We stood in my playroom, beside the dresser that had brought her there, and prayed for my brother, my family, and all that the day would hold.

After Michelle went home, without the dresser, my dad arrived and I gave him Dan's key. He left, and I waited. It was not long before he returned, and when I saw his face, I knew. He simply said, "He's gone."

My Brother

Let me tell you a little about Dan. Even as a child Dan was smart and had a great capacity to analyze and problem solve. He also had a strong will that tested my mother's patience when he was a toddler but served him well in the work world. Dan was one of the most intense individuals I have known and once compared himself to a pit bull, in an effort to name his tenacity. He struggled with depression as a child and addiction as a teen—those battles chased him into his adult life.

We grew up in a Christian home where we were loved. And although Dan made a profession of faith as a child, in his twenties he experienced God in a deep way and rearranged his life to follow after God. I remember him saying that it was God's kindness that won his heart. He was baptized, intently studied the Scriptures, sought wise counsel, and actively served. Dan and I shared an apartment during this season of his life.

But life is hard. We encounter challenges and suffering. Some of the struggles come from within and some come from outside of us, but regardless of their origin they can be overwhelming. Dan faced some significant challenges as he approached 30 years old, some resulting from his own choices but not all of them. When his efforts to fix what went wrong did not accomplish what he hoped, Dan resorted to escape through drugs and alcohol. He fell deeply into addiction, and he lost everything. And we thought we had lost Dan.

We fought for my brother, especially my parents. After a long, hard journey upward, including a 30-day treatment program in Arizona and years spent in a halfway-house in Florida, Dan moved back home shortly after my second daughter was born. He took a job as a purchaser for a small company. Although he still struggled with depression, he was respected professionally because of his work ethic, intellectual capacity, and respectful and honest dealings with his suppliers.

Dan loved my daughters, Hannah and Michaella, and his nephew, Sammy. He worked quite close to our home and would come over for lunch and a visit from time to time. The children drew out the best in my brother. Weeks before he died he told me that he would do anything for his nieces and nephew.

As is true for all of us, the temptations that are uniquely enticing to us have a way of creeping up. Dan's did as well. Those patterns steal away life because they seduce us into handling life on our own rather than depending on God. Not all of the consequences are deadly in the moment, but Dan's were. That August day Dan accidentally overdosed, and his heart stopped.

One afternoon weeks before, Dan and I were talking in my kitchen, and he spoke of the garbage can in his heart. He knew that it needed to be cleaned out before he could move forward in his healing. Despite belief in God and in the saving grace we are offered in Jesus, His Son, Dan was still stuck in his patterns of independence. The strength of his will—and he was strong-willed—was not enough to bring about healing and transformation.

We will not find perfection this side of heaven, but we can heal and find wholeness in God. God will clean out the garbage cans in our lives; He will disinfect our wounds. But we are given a choice—will we surrender ourselves to His care? For most of us the stakes do not appear to be as high as they were for my brother. Cleansing the wound stings, but it offers the hope of healing. God invites us to trust Him as Healer. Although it can be a daunting venture to face the infection and the messiness in our lives, it is worth the risk and the effort.

Light in the Darkness

I was not prepared to lose my brother, and I was not prepared for the journey of grief. I'm not sure that anyone ever is. I was taken off guard by the shock of Dan's death, the reality of profound loss, regrets, and all that followed. In those first weeks I had trouble sleeping, I wasn't hungry, and life seemed surreal, as though I was in a dream. I just couldn't believe Dan was gone. I remember saying to Michelle in the weeks after Dan's death that I had underestimated grief.

As the weeks turned into months, I realized that this journey of depletion and grief was my invitation to yield my own internal world and woundedness to the Divine Healer. God was present as my Comforter, but He also continued to reveal to me my own strategies for managing life that were independent of Him. I was aware of some of these strategies, such as my attachment to the approval of others, but my understanding grew deeper still. And I was not aware of some, such as how perfectionism and my attachment to being "right" had become my way of maintaining control and protecting myself. The process was humbling but it was healing to have God's light shine in these dark corners in my life.

There was a local small group that met for Bible study and prayer. I did not know the women well, but I knew that I needed a community. When I met with my counselor, I wondered aloud if it would be appropriate to ask if I could join the group and I voiced my hesitation. She said, "Just ask."

I was feeling fragile these days, and I could feel layers of insecurity and uncertainty stirring within me. I wanted to join this small group, but I feared rejection. In addition, I was anxious that these women would say yes simply because they "should," and I really wanted to be wanted. Ultimately, I had to trust God in my neediness. So I rallied my courage, and I asked. I was whole-heartedly welcomed into the group. Gratitude and relief welled up. Over the years these women have become a community of spiritual friends, giving and receiving.

A Time to Listen

Early in the summer as I struggled with depletion, my husband, Mark, had contacted a trusted friend and mentor in Texas, Preston Gillham. One hot July day I was running an errand at the mall, and as I pulled into the parking lot my phone rang. I couldn't imagine who might be calling at that time of day, and I did not recognize the number. But when I heard his unique Texan accent, I knew it was Pres. He offered wisdom and support in the weeks that followed, particularly following Dan's death. With Mark's encouragement, I asked Pres if I could visit. Once again I was reaching out to ask for the help I needed. Yes, uncomfortable. He and his wife, Dianne, graciously opened their home to me for a long weekend.

So in September I traveled to Texas to retreat and to spend time with God in the safety of the home of these friends. One afternoon as Pres and I talked, the events of recent months loomed large and my emotions were a tangled mess. I realized how small I felt. In the midst of all the loss and depletion, I longed to know what God thought of me and I ached for His affirmation. Pres challenged me to sit with God and ask Him what He called me.

I was afraid. I was afraid that if I asked God my question and He did not answer, I would be left worse off than when I started, feeling unworthy of a response. Or perhaps worse yet, I would, or could, fabricate an answer that was not truly the voice of God but my own thoughts within me. But I longed to hear God. So I retreated to the guest room where I had set up camp and I asked, and I listened.

As tears dripped down my cheeks, I asked God what He thought of me, and I waited. And I heard God speak. Within my heart He called me "Beautiful." He said, "You are becoming what I intend."

The darkness would continue to grow darker in the coming months, but I knew God was present. My friend Michelle, who had been my ally in this season of depletion and grief, continued to battle stage 4 breast cancer. Her health would diminish over the next year.

The first picture I share in this next section is an old one, but it reminds me of the waiting in dark seasons of our lives. Winter is a time when we do not see fruitfulness. It is fallow time. I struggle with these times where God calls us to patience, endurance, and trust. But God is working in the darkness; it is a chrysalis of sorts.

Invitation to Wait

I painted this chair in a sunny room on a winter day in 2000, the year I turned thirty. I had recently fallen in love and then experienced the disappointment of heartbreak. Despite God's confirmation of His purpose in this turn of events, I felt the grief of the loss of relationship but also the uncertainty of unrealized dreams. It was a tenuous and quiet place where I sensed God's presence, but He was silent.

In this season of transition I moved from the apartment I shared with my brother Dan and chose to live for a couple months in community at the L'Abri in Boston, founded by Francis and Edith Schaeffer. As I studied, worked, and lived among others, I asked those core questions that seem to surface at various seasons of our lives: "Who am I? And what is my purpose?"

I had not picked up my paintbrush in a long time, but in this reflective space I was drawn to my paints. The fog of uncertainty remained for over a year before God revealed the next significant step in my journey.

This image reminds me of God's invitation to be still with Him in the season of winter. Winter is a time when growth is not evident and many tree limbs are bare. It feels desolate as we await the return of visible life in spring. Life has not ceased...but this is a fallow time, a time of waiting. Although the darkness is longer in winter, the light does remain. I need to place myself in the light and trust as I wait.

Waiting certainly plays an enormous role in the unfolding story of God's relationship to man. It is God's oft repeated way of teaching us that His power is real and that He can answer our prayers without interference and manipulation from us. But we have such trouble getting our will, our time schedules out of the way.

Catherine Marshall, *Adventures in Prayer*

Invitation to Wait

*One thing I ask from the Lord, this only do I seek:
that I may dwell in the house of the Lord all the days of my life,
to gaze upon the beauty of the Lord and to seek him in his temple.*

*For in the day of trouble he will keep me safe in his dwelling;
he will hide me in the shelter of his sacred tent and set me high upon a rock.*

*Then my head will be exalted above the enemies who surround me;
at his sacred tent I will sacrifice with shouts of joy;*

*I will sing and make music to the Lord.
Hear my voice when I call, Lord; be merciful to me and answer me.
My heart says of you, "Seek his face!" Your face, Lord, I will seek.*

*Do not hide your face from me, do not turn your servant away in anger; you have been my helper.
Do not reject me or forsake me, God my Savior.*

*Though my father and mother forsake me, the Lord will receive me.
Teach me your way, Lord; lead me in a straight path because of my oppressors.*

*Do not turn me over to the desire of my foes,
for false witnesses rise up against me, spouting malicious accusations.*

*I remain confident of this: I will see the goodness of the Lord in the land of the living.
Wait for the Lord; be strong and take heart and wait for the Lord.*

Psalm 27:4-14

Christine 2000

Am I in
a winter
season?

• • • • •

Is God asking
me to wait
on Him and
to trust Him?

• • • • •

What could
God be
accomplishing
in the fallow
time that I
may not see?

Beyond the Walls

I drew this image in 2012 from a photo I found in a magazine a decade before. The image was intriguing to me when I first saw it, and this was actually the second time I had drawn it. I completed the first drawing years ago in black and white and gave it to my brother Dan. The lonely structure reminded me of him, but after he died I was unable to find the framed piece so I drew it again, in color this time.

The stone walls are the focus of this structure, and it feels closed. The walls speak to me of the ways we attempt to protect our hearts independently of God, our unique styles of self-sufficiency, or what some refer to as our false self. We choose ways of relating that are filled with striving rather than trusting. And one rock at a time we build walls that hide our vulnerable hearts—hearts that are uncertain of their value.

I place the rock of perfectionism in my castle wall as I attempt to appear flawless, although I know that the heart within bears scars and wounds as well as strength and health. I place the rock of pride in my wall as I seek to compare my worth to another and elevate myself through self-righteous judgment. As I seek the approval of others to define my identity and my value, I place another rock in my wall. There are countless rocks that I could have chosen to build my castle. My walls are unique to me. What are the rocks in your walls?

Within my self-protective structure lives a heart that longs for the light and craves freedom, the freedom God intended us to have in dependence on Him. He is dismantling my castle and setting my heart free.

The greatest accomplishment in life is to be what we are, which is God's idea of what He wanted us to be when he brought us into being...Accepting that gift is accepting God's will for us. And in its acceptance is found the path to growth and ultimate fulfillment.

Thomas Keating, *The Heart of the World*

The self that God persistently loves is not my prettied-up pretend self but my actual self—the real me. But, master of delusion that I am, I have trouble penetrating my web of self deceptions and knowing this real me. I continually confuse it with some ideal self I wish I were. The roots of our pretend self lie in our childhood discovery that we can secure love by presenting ourselves in the most flattering light.

David Benner, *The Gift of Being Yourself*

Beyond the Walls

"My people have committed two sins: They have forsaken me, the spring of living water, and have dug their own cisterns, broken cisterns that cannot hold water."

Jeremiah 2:13

Christine

What rocks have I placed in my walls?

• • • • • •

Are there windows in my walls that allow me to glimpse the Light?

Journey into Christ

Darkness. Turmoil. Fragmented pieces. Chaos.

Swirling blackness. Dark and heavy marks. Shadowy shapes of dingy color, lacking clarity. The background of this image speaks to me of the times and seasons when I am off center, out of balance, and frazzled. Colors are hinted at, and there is shape to the objects that are spinning but...

The whirling, messy turmoil is a stark contrast to the clear, colorful image of the cross.

The shapes come together, held within the cross. The colors are clear and true.

In this place of the cross, there is re-creation. In the place of repentance, the fragments come together as a whole. In the place of death to self, light replaces darkness and the muddied colors become clear and true. In the place of abiding in Jesus the Son of God, His light and design are evident, and there is wholeness.

For he has rescued us from the dominion of darkness and brought us into the kingdom of the Son he loves, in whom we have redemption, the forgiveness of sins.

The Son is the image of the invisible God, the firstborn over all creation. For in him all things were created: things in heaven and on earth, visible and invisible, whether thrones or powers or rulers or authorities; all things have been created through him and for him.

He is before all things, and in him all things hold together.

Colossians 1:13-17

Journey into Christ

I have been crucified with Christ and I no longer live, but Christ lives in me.

The life I now live in the body, I live by faith in the Son of God, who loved me and gave himself for me.

Galatians 2:20

What feels messy and chaotic in me?

• • • • • •

Can I still the outer chaos in my life to acknowledge the inner chaos?

• • • • •

Can I see a hint of the good in me? What would God do if I yielded the spinning fragments to Him?

Invitation to Dependence

One day when Hannah was three years old, she sat in the living room playing with her blocks. I was working around the house, perhaps in the kitchen, but when I looked in on her I was struck by what she had built. She had worked out her faith in her play and built a cross.

There is simplicity to a child's faith and a willingness to trust. So often, children are wholehearted.

A child will ask for affection and for help with ease and humility. They are also disarmingly honest about what they think and feel, lacking the pretense that we gain over the years.

How can I maintain a childlike receptivity to God? How can I remember that I am the child and I am under authority, dependent on my Father's care? Jesus, who was God, took the position of Son, placing Himself under authority. How can I embrace the command to be like a child?

At that time the disciples came to Jesus and asked, "Who, then, is the greatest in the kingdom of heaven?"

He called a little child to him, and placed the child among them.

And he said: "Truly I tell you, unless you change and become like little children, you will never enter the kingdom of heaven.

Therefore, whoever takes the lowly position of this child is the greatest in the kingdom of heaven.

And whoever welcomes one such child in my name welcomes me."

Matthew 18:1-5

Surely I have composed and quieted my soul;
like a weaned child rests against his mother,
my soul is like a weaned child within me.

Psalm 131:2 NASB

Like a Child, 2012

Can I offer
God my
simple faith?

● ● ● ● ● ●

How is God
inviting me to
come to Him
like a child?

Invitation to Listen

One morning my daughter was up early. She brought her Bible downstairs and curled up in the large refinished pine chair in the living room. She started reading. She and I had been praying that she would learn to listen to God from her heart.

This image reminds me of our need to turn our attention to God, to His Word, and to seek to listen with our hearts.

A couple years ago I read Ruth Haley Barton's book *Sacred Rhythms*. I was familiar with many of the spiritual practices that she described, but the ancient practice of lectio divina was new to me and I was intrigued.

Lectio divina means divine reading, and it is a practice intended to create space to respond to God from our hearts. A passage of Scripture is chosen, usually 6-8 verses, or a story account. The passage is then read in four readings with four minutes of silence between each reading. One intentionally seeks to listen for the Holy Spirit's movement in the silence.

In the first reading focus on being attentive—what is the word or phrase that stands out? The second reading is for reflection, and I ponder how my life is touched by the word that is given. In the third reading we respond to God. What is my response to the word that is given? And in the fourth reading one rests in the presence of God.

I waited patiently for the Lord; and He inclined to me and heard my cry.
How blessed is the man who has made the Lord his trust…

Many, O Lord my God, are the wonders which You have done, and Your thoughts toward us; there is none to compare with You.

If I would declare and speak of them, they would be too numerous to count.
Sacrifice and meal offering You have not desired; my ears You have opened;
burnt offering and sin offering You have not required.

Then I said, "Behold, I come; in the scroll of the book it is written of me.
I delight to do Your will, O my God; Your Law is within my heart."

Psalm 40:1, 4a, 5-8 NASB

Let the word of Christ richly dwell within you…

Colossians 3:16a NASB

When I read the Bible, how can I listen with my heart, as well as my mind?

Listen

Traveling Together

This drawing was completed when I spent a long weekend in Texas with friends. I had boldly asked if I could visit. I needed to rest, retreat, and be with God. These friends offered me hospitality, their authentic selves, prayer, and a willingness to listen.

This drawing of my girls is from a photo of when Hannah was two years old and Michaella was just a wee one, brand new.

Our relationship as brothers and sisters in the body of Christ is an eternal bond. We are connected by the blood of Christ. And by design we need one another.

In my family of origin I am the "big sister," the oldest of five kids, and watching over my siblings was familiar to me. In this season I needed to learn to rely on others in a deeper way and to trust God in receiving care from my brothers and sisters by faith.

I remember my counselor saying to me when I crashed that summer that it takes a deeper humility to receive service than to give it. She asked me how I would respond if my church offered to bring meals for our family. Well, my Sunday school class did offer to bring meals, and we accepted the gift. It was humbling, but significant, to receive care from the body of Christ. The day my brother died a friend had already been on the calendar to bring a meal for us. God provides abundantly for our needs, often through His people.

Two are better than one, because they have a good return for their labor:

If either of them falls down, one can help the other up.

But pity anyone who falls and has no one to help them up.

Also, if two lie down together, they will keep warm. But how can one keep warm alone?

Though one may be overpowered, two can defend themselves.

A cord of three strands is not quickly broken.

Ecclesiastes 4:9-12

Feeling Together

Just as a body, though one, has many parts, but all its many parts form one body, so it is with Christ.... But God has put the body together, giving greater honor to the parts that lacked it, so that there should be no division in the body, but that its parts should have equal concern for each other. If one part suffers, every part suffers with it; if one part is honored, every part rejoices with it. Now you are the body of Christ, and each one of you is a part of it.

1 Corinthians 12:12, 24b-27

Sisters, 2009

What does it mean to me to be a brother or sister?

• • • • • •

Do I need to ask for help?

• • • • • •

Do I need to offer help?

Not My Way But Yours

I started reading the C. S. Lewis books, *The Chronicles of Narnia,* to my girls. When we read *Prince Caspian,* my heart was touched by Lucy's late night encounter with Aslan. The story painted a picture of God's gentle conviction and Lucy's surrender and empowerment.

> *"Oh dear, oh dear," said Lucy. "And I was so pleased to find you again. And I thought you'd let me stay. And I thought you'd come roaring in and frighten all the enemies away— like last time. And now everything is going to be horrid."*
>
> *"It is hard for you, little one," said Aslan. "But things never happen the same way twice. It has been hard for us all in Narnia before now."*
>
> *Lucy buried her head in his mane to hide from his face. But there must have been magic in his mane. She could feel lion-strength going into her. Quite suddenly she sat up.*
>
> *"I'm sorry, Aslan," she said, "I'm ready now."*
>
> *"Now you are a lioness," said Aslan.*

In 2010 my friend Michelle faced numerous setbacks as she battled cancer. She fought hard. I prayed, her family prayed, perhaps thousands prayed. I knew that God could heal her. We believed in God's healing power.

But there came a time in the summer of 2010 when I began to wonder if God's purpose was something other than healing. Michelle was a devoted follower of Christ, a wife and mother, one of my closest friends, and a gifted woman with influence beyond what I even knew. Why would God take her home? Surrender is hard.

Not My Way But Yours

Consider it all joy, my brethren, when you encounter various trials, knowing that the testing of your faith produces endurance.

And let endurance have its perfect result, so that you may be perfect and complete, lacking in nothing.

James 1:2-4 NASB

Beloved, do not be surprised at the fiery ordeal among you, which comes upon you for your testing, as though some strange thing were happening to you; but to the degree that you share the sufferings of Christ, keep on rejoicing; so that also at the revelation of His glory you may rejoice with exultation.

1 Peter 4:12-13 NASB

Leaning In, Holding On, and Aligning to the Rhythm of His Heart, 2012

Has God revealed truth to me in a story?

• • • • • •

What are the meaningful adventures, conversations, and moments of my story?

• • • • • •

Does this encounter between Lucy and Aslan speak to me?

*I will give you the treasures of darkness
and hidden wealth of secret places, so that
you may know that it is I, the Lord, the
God of Israel, who calls you by your name.*

Isaiah 45:3 NASB

Treasures in the Darkness

Loss of a Friend

The spiritual direction training program that I was prayerfully considering would begin in the fall of 2011 at Kairos: School of Spiritual Formation. As I sought discernment, I planned to attend several retreats in the 2010-2011 year of Kairos. The retreats would give me the opportunity to experience the school, and my first retreat, Visualizing Your Spiritual Journey, was in September.

I looked forward to that September weekend—it felt like a ray of sunshine breaking through a sky that had been cloudy for a long time. But just as there are often glimpses of sunshine while the thunder rumbles and the rain pours, so it was that September.

My friend Michelle, my ally and a kindred spirit, had fought breast cancer for over three years, and in recent weeks her body had been shutting down. She was in her last days of life here, and her battle with an invisible enemy was coming to an end. I saw her one last time two days before I left for the retreat.

I had known that Michelle was in a serious battle for her health from the beginning. When she told me the diagnosis of "stage 4 cancer," I had searched the Internet for meaning and discovered that the odds were against her. But I believed in a God who was able to heal and who often did heal. Now, more than three years later, I could barely grasp the fact that God was not going to "fix" Michelle's broken body in this world.

God, in His infinite wisdom, took Michelle home to be with Him on September 14, 2010. She was a courageous, godly woman, one of the most self-aware and perceptive people I have known. Michelle was a great mom to her three boys, partner to her husband, and a natural leader. I could not even comprehend the grief of her husband and her boys, and yet I knew God was with them.

And for myself, I had lost a sister and an ally, a friend who was compassionate and honest. I loved Michelle. My heart ached, and I told God that this felt like too much.

That year, as grief overshadowed my life, I attended the Visualizing Your Spiritual Journey retreats at Kairos in September, November, January, and March. The idea of using creativity in my prayer intrigued me. That first weekend, when Michelle was in her last days, my heart was overwhelmed with great sadness and full of questions without answers. The invitation to use colors and creativity to place my heart before God felt fitting—my prayer could be messy and intense.

Finding Treasures

That fall my life remained under the shadow of grief. The loss of my brother was still tangible, and this new loss ached. Yet, as I continued to listen for God, I saw sparks of light.

My husband sent me an e-mail from work one day with a quote from our friend Pres:
> Life is full of dark times: when questions multiply like rabbits and answers are few and far between, emotions screech, and anguish occupies the front row in your mind's theatre...Isaiah says, "I will give you the treasures of darkness and hidden wealth of secret places, so that you may know that it is I, the Lord, the God of Israel, who calls you by name." (45:3) Darkness holds fortunes of faith that the daylight can't reveal. Calm down and relax. Embrace the darkness and listen for the Lord. He is there and will use the darkness to invest treasures in your life that are inconceivable right now.

I was willing to embrace the darkness, trusting in my Father God who called me by name.

The retreats at the Jesuit Center were healing and watered the seed of creativity within me. My soul found space to listen, grieve, create, and heal in the silence of those weekends. The beauty quieted me, and I felt God's presence. Sometimes the quiet allowed the turmoil or angst that had been pressed down beneath the conscious level to surface. And there I offered it to God.

In the past, on occasion, I would pull out paper and paints to process and create, but I did not see it as a part of my life's work. As individuals in the Kairos community began to respond to my drawings and resonate with the images, I heard God's invitation to embrace this gift and allow it to be a tool in His hand. What are the unique gifts within you? When do you feel a sense of rightness, joy, and energy in your work?

I began to see glimpses of the treasures hidden in the darkness. My heart still ached as spring came, but I saw new life sprouting and sparks of light. I made application to enter the Spiritual Direction Training program, and I was accepted. Adventures were before me.

Offering the Pain

My first weekend retreat at Kairos will always stand out in my memory because of Michelle.

Through cancer I watched Michelle's faith grow stronger as she fought for her life and as her body grew frail. Michelle's love for Jesus and confidence that she was loved by God expanded through suffering. That weekend I envisioned her being called home from active duty to hear the words, "Well done, good and faithful servant" from her Savior and Lord.

Michelle and I shared a deep friendship. Bryan, Michelle's husband, once commented that Michelle and I did not shop for shoes together. We enjoyed sharing a cup of coffee and deep conversation—now, when I sit down to be with Abba God, I often use the mug in my cupboard that was her favorite. As iron sharpens iron, so we supported each other's journey into deeper intimacy with God. Michelle had been a friend through some of my darkest days, and as I started to research this calling of spiritual direction I realized that Michelle intuitively listened and loved as a spiritual companion.

My tears were many that weekend. I prayed for Michelle, as she entered the presence of the Savior she loved; I prayed for her husband and three boys; and I prayed for myself. Probably thousands had prayed for Michelle. But Father God took her home on September 14th, and her suffering came to an end.

The core of my prayer that weekend was that God would redeem the pain and the loss. My heart longed for God to bring beauty out of darkness and life out of suffering. Our retreat project was to create an invitation to God. This was mine...different from my usual style because this was messy and emotional, painful and sad. Yet God's grace was evident even still.

After you have suffered for a little while, the God of all grace, who called you to His eternal glory in Christ, will Himself perfect, confirm, strengthen, and establish you.

1 Peter 5:10 NASB

Come, let us return to the Lord. He has torn us to pieces but he will heal us; he has injured us but he will bind up our wounds.

After two days he will revive us; on the third day he will restore us, that we may live in his presence.

Let us acknowledge the Lord; let us press on to acknowledge him. As surely as the sun rises, he will appear; he will come to us like the winter rains, like the spring rains that water the earth.

Hosea 6:1-3

Prayer, 2010

What are
the most
significant
losses of
my life?

• • • • • •

Are there tears
that whisper
to me of losses
I have not
acknowledged?

• • • • • •

What do I
need in order
to lean into
God's love in
the midst of
my grief?

Beauty on the Journey

Saturday afternoon on my first Kairos weekend, I wandered outside when there was some time to reflect. I noticed a tree between the building and the parking lot. I am not sure what prompted me to explore because it did not appear impressive, although it was quite large. But as I drew near, I saw a place where the branches reached low to the ground and they seemed to part, becoming a doorway.

I entered the tree, and I sensed I had entered a sacred place. In His creation God provided a sanctuary, a place set apart to listen. I felt held by the arms of this grand old sentry who seemed to stand watch, and I listened for God's voice.

The gnarly, twisted old tree was beautiful, full of life and strength. It was not refined, elegant, or pristine, but rather raw, real, scarred...and beautiful. The tree had a story to tell, for it had stood the test of time.

The experience and the image were strikingly redemptive. I thought about how Jesus heals our wounds, gives us strength to endure, and walks with us through suffering. Healing often leaves scars, and I wonder if that is by divine intent—I expect it is. Perhaps some scars remain as badges of courage, to bear witness of battles endured and wounds healed. The scarred trunk and the tangled limbs were a testimony to endurance, patience, and growth. It has been told that lightening hit this tree in recent years. Storms have come and gone, seasons have changed, and one year follows another, but the tree stands.

Our growth and uniquely created beauty is revealed as we allow the life of Christ and God's hand to bring healing, to enable us to endure suffering, and through time, to renew strength and turn wounds into scars. Jesus will bear His scars for all eternity, and I think there is something profound in that.

"But blessed is the one who trusts in the Lord,
whose confidence is in him.

They will be like a tree planted by the water
that sends out its roots by the stream.

It does not fear when heat comes;
its leaves are always green.

It has no worries in a year of drought
and never fails to bear fruit"....

Heal me, Lord, and I will be healed;
save me and I will be saved,
for you are the one I praise.

Jeremiah 17:7-8, 14

We will love our story only to the degree that we see the glory that seeps through our most significant shattering. To see that glory, we must enter into and read our tragedies with confidence that they will end better than we could ever imagine.... Because we live in a fallen world, we will encounter abandonment, betrayal, and shame. These experiences are inevitable, but they also provide the necessary context for coming to grips with how we will live our lives. In the midst of affliction, we become either our truest or most false self.

Dan Allender, *To Be Told*

Life, 2010

Do I see myself as gnarly and scarred?

· · · · · ·

Do I see the beauty in God's design of me?

· · · · · ·

Have I allowed God to heal raw wounds into scars, badges of courage?

A Place to Listen

There are so many times when we need to be with God. Perhaps we face a decision and our hearts long for discernment; perhaps we have done wrong and we need to repent; or perhaps we just need to be with Him.

The small rooms at the Jesuit Retreat Center provide a sacred space for stillness. It is in that quiet space, set apart for listening, that I often find discernment, healing, and hope. From that quiet place I gain a perspective of myself and of the outside world. Then, I can move into my world with greater love and freedom because I have been with God.

Often God gives us the gift of a place, or places, where the air is thin and somehow it seems easier to listen and be present to the One who loves us most. Although God is present in all places, we have trouble being present to Him in all places.

I love the Jesuit Center when I have the opportunity to retreat for a weekend, but in the day-to-day I find a walk outside or time in my chair in my living room by the window can provide what is needed.

What do you need to be intentionally present to God? Do you need quiet or beauty? Do you need an orderly space? Look for those places where you can be attentive to God. It could be a special chair in your home, a park, or a place of retreat. Regardless of where that place is, it is imperative that we set aside time to be with Him.

Let us say it again: The universal Presence is a fact. God is here. The whole universe is alive with His life. And He is no strange or foreign God, but the familiar Father of our Lord Jesus Christ whose love has for these thousands of years enfolded the sinful race of men. And always He is trying to get our attention, to reveal Himself to us, to communicate with us. We have within us the ability to know Him if we will but respond to His overtures.... We will know Him in increasing degree as our receptivity becomes more perfect by faith, love, and practice.

A. W. Tozer, *The Pursuit of God*

Always, everywhere God is present, and always He seeks to discover Himself to each one. He would reveal not only that He is, but what He is as well.

A. W. Tozer, *The Pursuit of God*

Place to Listen

"Praise be to the name of God for ever and ever; wisdom and power are his.

He changes times and seasons; he deposes kings and raises up others.

He gives wisdom to the wise and knowledge to the discerning.

He reveals deep and hidden things; he knows what lies in darkness, and light dwells with him."

Daniel 2:20-22

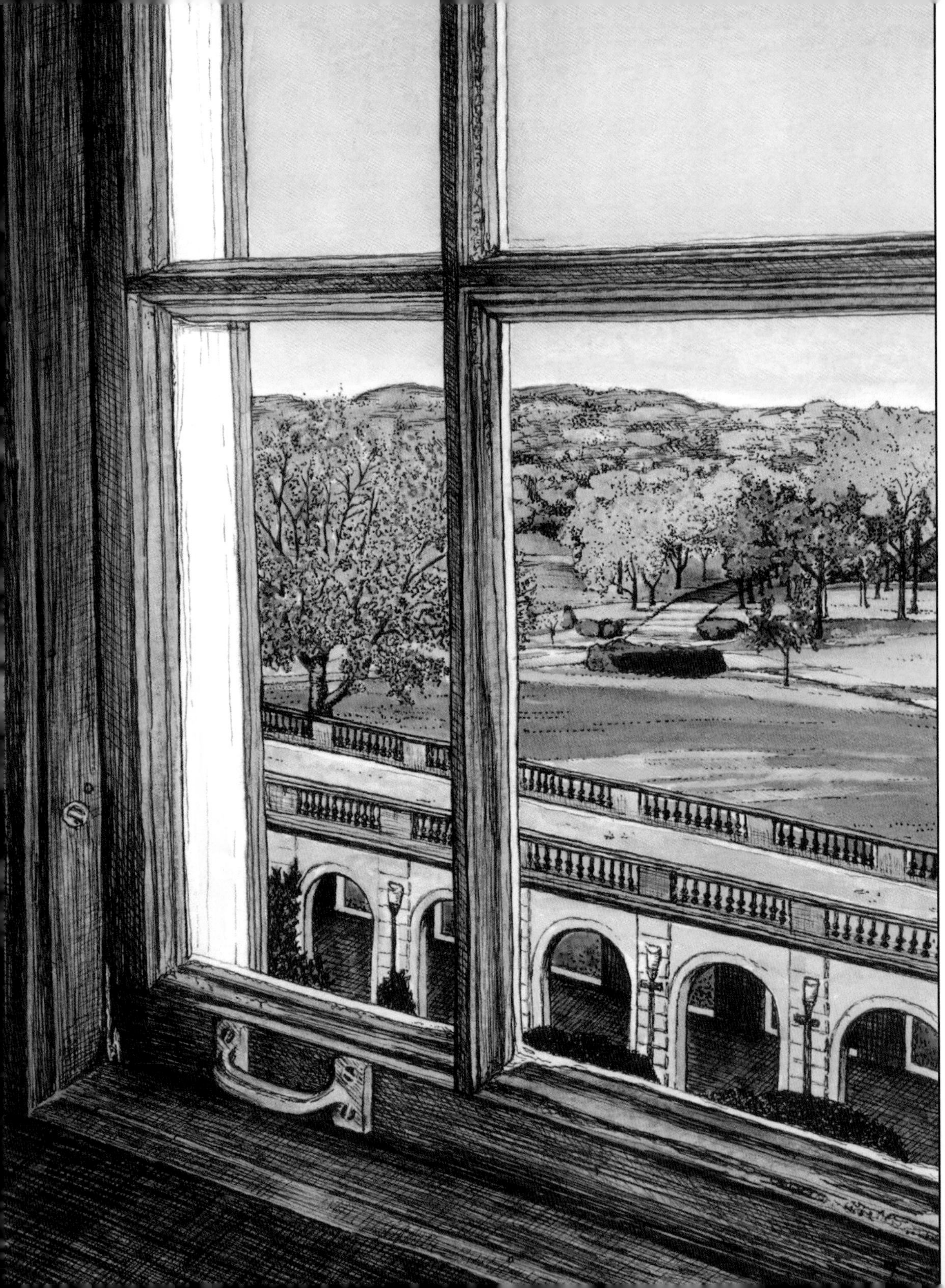

Perspective, 2012

What do
I need in
order to be
present to
God, to be
open and
attentive?

・・・・・・

Is there a
place for me
where the
air is thin
and I am
most present
to God?

A Place to Listen

Journey of Grief

There is something infinitely hopeful about the coming of dawn. The darkness has passed, and with the slow arrival of morning new hope is stirred. Warmth begins to creep over the land, the birds sing, and the night flees. Light grows from a soft distant glow to burning clarity on a cloudless day.

There are seasons of the soul that seem marked by darkness. Sometimes grief casts a shadow of darkness over the soul. Suffering and pain can bring darkness with them as well. As a friend once said to me, when the darkness has been particularly long or painful, the coming of dawn can ignite joy that burns your soul.

When my brother passed away, and then Michelle, I intentionally embraced the season of grief. I created space to feel and lament, to be with God in the loss. Jerry Sittser, an author who experienced catastrophic loss, described an image that has stuck with me in his book, *A Grace Disguised*. If you chase after the setting sun you may never reach the dawn, but if you enter the darkness you will meet the sun as it rises. There came a time when I felt joy stir and I could see light, dim as it seemed at first. The stirring of energy and hope are celebrated when dawn finally appears. I am grateful for the dawn.

"Grief has carved out deep places in my heart. Father, pour yourself in. I know You long to fill me with Yourself. I am willing to receive, I long to receive...more of You." Christine, journal entry

My soul is downcast within me.

Yet this I call to mind and therefore I have hope:
Because of the Lord's great love we are not consumed,
for his compassions never fail. They are new every morning;
great is your faithfulness.

I say to myself, "The Lord is my portion; therefore I will wait for him."

The Lord is good to those whose hope is in him, to the one who seeks him;
it is good to wait quietly for the salvation of the Lord.

Lamentations 3:20b-26

Journey of Grief

Therefore, do not throw away
your confidence, which has a
great reward. For you have need
of endurance, so that when you
have done the will of God, you
may receive what was promised....

But my righteousness one shall live
by faith.

Hebrews 10:35-36, 38a NASB

Morning Has Come, 2013

Is there a darkness in my life that has not yet seen the dawn?

● ● ● ● ● ●

Do I trust that darkness is not forever and that morning will come?

Vision on the Journey

This image is a reworking of my black and white drawing *Becoming*.

In January 2011 I attended a weekend retreat at Kairos for creating and listening to God. I was asking God for confirmation of the call to spiritual direction I had heard a year and a half before. That year and a half was filled with challenges and loss, but I heard His invitation to trust and to yield to His hand.

Now, after a season of autumn loss and after the seeming sleep of winter, I could feel spring stirring. God was calling me to new things. Thus the image is filled with color, and to me, it is filled with hope and vision. There is a small tear in the wing of the butterfly because the past seasons have a cost, but life and brilliance are far more present in the image than the darkness.

During the opening service that weekend at Kairos, a quote was shared that seemed to echo my heart: "New life is often preceded by a breaking down, a stripping away, so that there is space to be open to the new" (Marcus Pomeroy, Spiritual Director, Advent Retreat, Kairos).

Then the Lord answered me and said,
"Record the vision and inscribe it on tablets,
that the one that reads it may run.

For the vision is yet for the appointed time;
it hastens toward the goal, and it will not fail.

Though it tarries, wait for it;
for it will certainly come, it will not delay."

Habakkuk 2:2-3 NASB

On the Journey

Hand your dream over to God, and then leave it in his keeping. There seem to be periods when the dream is like a seed that must be planted in the dark earth and left there to germinate. This is not a time of possessiveness on our part. There are things we can and must do—fertilizing, watering, weeding—hard work and self-discipline. But the growth of that seed, the mysterious and irresistible burgeoning of life in dark and in secret, that is God's part in the process.

Catherine Marshall,
Adventures in Prayer

Vision, 2011

Is there
a dream
stirring in
my heart?

• • • • • •

Is there a
calling on
my life that
I am to pay
attention to?

• • • • • •

Is God
calling me to
something
new?

Visions on the Journey

Invitation to Stillness

"Be still [cease striving], *and know that I am God." Psalm 46:10*

We live in a culture that is hurried and busy. More often than not if you ask a friend or an acquaintance, "How are you?" you will hear the response, "Busy!"

There are so many layers to our lives. Technology can infiltrate moments that at one time were quiet and reflective. The pace of our world seems to be continually accelerating. And the goal of productivity has been placed high above many other values. Even our leisure time can be exhausting.

Externally and internally we are often harried and stressed. There is a chaos that cries out for stillness, rest, and order.

I was drawn to a photograph I took one weekend of the porch of the Jesuit Center. The space in the image felt calm, reflective, and inviting. There is an interesting tension between the two spaces. For me it is an invitation—to be still, to gain perspective, to listen.

This is what the Lord says: "Stand at the crossroads and look; ask for the ancient paths, ask where the good way is, and walk in it, and you will find rest for your souls."

Jeremiah 6:16a

"Be still [cease striving], and know that I am God.
I will be exalted among the nations,
I will be exalted in the earth."
The Lord Almighty is with us.

Psalm 46:10-11a

Where am I striving rather than abiding?

· · · · · ·

What will happen if I still the spinning in my mind and let go of the mental striving?

· · · · · ·

What do I notice in me when I become still and attentive to God?

What Are You Doing Here?

My small group practiced lectio divina with the story in Scripture of Elijah's journey to Mt. Hebron to meet with God.

At the big showdown between Elijah and the prophets of Baal, God decisively revealed Himself and the victory was evident before the people of Israel. The prophets of Baal were killed, and God lifted the drought He had placed over the land. But Queen Jezebel was enraged and threatened to kill Elijah.

Despite the obvious victory, Elijah is exhausted and discouraged. Physical fatigue, fear, and uncertainty drive Elijah to pursue God. After sleep, and being fed by an angel of the Lord, Elijah journeys 40 days to Mt. Hebron and settles into a cave. God asks him, "What are you doing here?"

God tells Elijah that He will come to him. There is a violent wind that breaks the rocks, but the Scripture tells us that God is not in the wind. There is a mighty earthquake, but the Scripture tells us that God is not in the earthquake. Then there is a fire, but God is not in the fire. Finally, a gentle whisper, or a still small voice, or the sound of sheer silence, and Elijah wraps his face in his cloak and goes out of the cave to be with God.

The stillness where God comes to us is striking. The question God asks echoes in my heart. This story was simmering in my soul the day I had an appointment to meet with my spiritual director. So with a little over an hour, I sat down with my watercolor pencils, paint, and pastels. I asked God to create with me. The rough outline was defined in that prayer time, and I completed the drawing in the following days. The question still echoes in my soul: *What are you doing here?*

And the word of the Lord came to him: "What are you doing here, Elijah?"

He replied, "I have been very zealous for the Lord God Almighty. The Israelites have rejected your covenant, torn down your altars, and put your prophets to death with the sword. I am the only one left, and now they are trying to kill me too."

The Lord said, "Go out and stand on the mountain in the presence of the Lord, for the Lord is about to pass by."

Then a great and powerful wind tore the mountains apart and shattered the rocks before the Lord, but the Lord was not in the wind. After the wind there was an earthquake, but the Lord was not in the earthquake. After the earthquake came a fire, but the Lord was not in the fire. And after the fire came a gentle whisper.

1 Kings 19:9b-12

What Are You Doing Here?

We are starved for Mystery, to know this God as one who is totally other and to experience reverence in His presence. We are starved for intimacy, to see, feel and know God in the very cells of our being. We are starved for rest, to know God beyond what we can do for Him. We are starved for quiet, to hear the sound of sheer silence that is the presence of God Himself.

Ruth Haley Barton, *Invitation to Solitude and Silence*

What is needed when my body is fatigued and I am depleted?

・・・・・・

Where do I go when I notice that my soul is weary?

・・・・・・

Where do I turn when I feel despair and oppression?

Trust in the Lord with all your heart and
lean not on your own understanding;
in all your ways submit to him, and he
will direct your paths.

Proverbs 3:5-6

Transformed Through Surrender

Spiritual Direction Training Begins

In the fall of 2011, I began the two year spiritual direction training program at Kairos. Once a month I traveled to the Jesuit Retreat Center in Wernersville for the weekend. I expected that I would be trained to attentively listen to the heart of another and that I would be encouraged to be attentive to God as I companioned that individual in their walk with God. But I did not realize how much of the program would invite me to simply listen for God and bask in His love myself. And as I listened, God gently put His divine finger on those areas of my life where He wanted to set me free.

Friday morning of that first weekend, as I prepared to leave for Wernersville, everything was difficult. I woke up with a headache that threatened to derail my plans. Although my husband offered to drive me to the retreat center, I sent him to work, praying the headache would lift. Mark's kindness and support had encouraged me all along the way. I misplaced my glasses in the chaos of packing, and then I realized Mark had accidentally picked up my cell phone as well as his own. Stress and anxiety had me wound tight, but I finally got on the road.

Two hours later as I drove through the gate to the retreat center, I felt my body relax. Peace washed over me, and I knew I was where God intended me to be. I found my way to my room, a little cubicle with a bed, desk, chair, simple wardrobe, and large old window. The retreat center, that had once been a seminary, was quiet. I was ready to pay attention.

The sense of anticipation was tangible that first training weekend as our class of fifteen students gathered. From the beginning our instructors, Marcus, Peg, and Cheryl, invited us to notice what was moving in our souls and to be attentive to God's movement within us. This was the place to begin because we cannot lead another person any farther than we have traveled ourselves in the journey. So, much of this training would involve doing our own work and following the Spirit's lead as God drew us into deeper surrender.

Friday afternoon we gathered around a table filled with pictures of all sorts. Our task was to notice what picture drew our attention and seemed to echo the state of our soul. I chose a photo of an older man, a grandfather figure, seated in a chair while holding the hands of a toddler as he took his first steps. The grandfather's posture and expression was protective, and yet delighted, as he watched the courageous steps of the child. Although tentative and wobbly, joy lit up the child's face as he stepped out. I felt like that child stepping out under the watchful care of the One who loved me.

Surrender

I have always handled life predominantly with my mind. But that is not all that we are. God created us: heart, soul, mind, and body. And however one tries to define the different facets of our being, our life's journey involves trusting God with our whole self. It is in the surrender of our whole person that God works the beautiful transformation that sets us free.

Because of my unique personality and history, I often problem solved analytically. It is not that emotions do not influence me, for they certainly do, but in a subversive way. Through training I learned to recognize more clearly how those feelings in my gut were indicators to me of blind spots and hidden desires—entrusted to God they became allies. They acted like little spies hinting at the happenings in my heart. With these new revelations, the echoes of untruth could be released and the activity of God could be embraced. I also began to understand more clearly that when my mind started spinning I was not being controlled by the Spirit but by my own strategies for managing life. I wanted to live a life in union with God where I was free to love and serve as God intended.

In those coming months as we studied, interacted, and practiced, God had a way of identifying those things He wanted to address. At times my emotions would spike with intensity as He took me back into my past, bringing something to the surface that He wanted to address. Sometimes God would reveal my insecurity and invite me to deeper trust and greater courage. Sometimes He would reveal my sin and independence and invite me to repentance. My self-knowledge increased, and "letting go" became a strong pattern in my life. Has God placed His finger on something in your life, inviting you to surrender? Do you see His desire for you to receive the depths of His love?

As the months went by I felt a shift within me. I was more aware of how the niggling feelings that surfaced told me something about me, and although I may have observed something true in someone else I could leave the other in God's hands and choose to do my own work. Early on Sunday morning that first weekend, before breakfast, I sat down with oil pastels and played. I drew a butterfly coming out of its chrysalis, as a night sky was transformed by the light.

Surrender to His Hands

The Potter places the clay on the wheel and sets the wheel in motion. At His command the wheel begins to spin.

The wheel spins and strong unyielding hands apply firm pressure to the lump of clay. Round and round the wheel whirls. He presses into the center, and His hands create a well. The clay yields to steady strength. The Potter's hands press and pull, and the clay takes form, spinning through purposeful fingers.

Do the hands of God press deep and pull high to create a vessel to fill with more of Himself? Will I yield to the discomfort of being transformed?

One week as my small group practiced lectio, we used the Scripture that describes God as the Potter. The powerful image caught my attention, and I wanted to draw the hands of the Potter working. I discovered a local potter and asked if I could take pictures while he worked on the wheel.

Interestingly, as I drew the image, I had the most trouble rendering the bowl that the potter was creating. It was not cooperating. I started to wonder, how often do we climb off the wheel and try to tell God what needs to be done in our lives? Does God sit back and wait for us to surrender and trust Him?

There is immense significance in the fact that we are created— we have a designer. A plate cannot pour liquid like a pitcher does, and a mug is rather useless to hold a sandwich. Am I living true to my design? How can I yield intentionally to the hands of God as He seeks to work in my life?

Yet you, Lord, are our Father.
We are the clay, you are the potter;
we are all the work of your hand.

Isaiah 64:8

Surrender is foundational to Christian spirituality and is the soil out of which obedience should grow. Christ does not simply want our compliance. He wants our heart. He wants our love and he offers us his. He invites us to surrender to his love.

David Benner,
Surrender to Love

Woe to those who go to great depths
to hide their plans from the Lord,
who do their work in darkness and think,
"Who sees us? Who will know?"

You turn things upside down,
as if the potter were thought to be like the clay!
Shall what is formed say to the one who formed it,
"You did not make me"?
Can the pot say to the potter,
"You know nothing"?

Isaiah 29:15-16

Surrender to His Hand

The Potter's Hands, 2012

What does it mean that I am the clay and God is the Potter?

. . . . . .

Do I feel the pressure of His hand pressing the clay?

. . . . . .

Do I see myself as a work of art created by the Master?

A Bold Request

Do you ever long for more of God, this One who is so far beyond us? Do you desire to see Him more clearly and know Him more intimately? Moses was a man who listened when God spoke. I am drawn to the story of Moses, and I am captured by his friendship with God.

The story of Moses begins with danger and failure. As a baby, Moses would have been killed with the other Israelite baby boys as ordered by Pharaoh, but in God's providence his life was entrusted to Pharaoh's daughter and he grew up in the royal household.

As a young man, Moses recoiled at the abuse of his brothers, the people of Israel, enslaved by Pharaoh. One day, enraged by the oppression he observed, he murdered an Egyptian slave driver. Fearing for his life, he fled Egypt and disappeared into the wilderness for forty years.

But God had not forgotten Moses. God called this man, an apparent failure, to lead His people out of slavery and into freedom. Moses resisted the call, wrestling with his own insecurity, and yet he obeyed. He became a man God referred to as friend—a man who followed God, communed with Him, and led His people with compassion and integrity. What transformed Moses from an insecure desert shepherd to a man who led a nation and boldly asked God to reveal Himself?

I am humbled at God's willingness to stoop low to allow Himself to be known, even in part. And I wonder at that dark place in the cleft of the rock where God placed Moses under His hand to protect him. How dark was it and how did it feel? How silent was that space?

As we ask God for more of Himself, are there dark places in our lives that hold the same waiting before the wonder?

A Bold Request

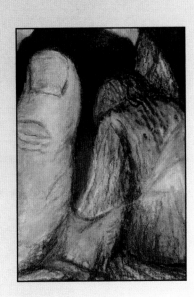

The Lord replied, "My Presence will go with you, and I will give you rest."

Then Moses said to him, "If your Presence does not go with us, do not send us up from here...."

And the Lord said to Moses, "I will do the very thing you have asked, because I am pleased with you and I know you by name."

Then Moses said, "Now show me your glory."

And the Lord said, "I will cause all my goodness to pass in front of you, and I will proclaim my name, the Lord, in your presence. I will have mercy on whom I will have mercy, and I will have compassion on whom I will have compassion. But," he said, "you cannot see my face, for no one may see me and live."

Then the Lord said, "There is a place near me where you may stand on a rock. When my glory passes by, I will put you in a cleft in the rock and cover you with my hand until I have passed by. Then I will remove my hand and you will see my back; but my face must not be seen."

Exodus 33:14-15, 17-23

With the veil removed by the rending of Jesus' flesh, with nothing on God's side to prevent us from entering, why do we tarry without? Why do we consent to abide all our days just outside the Holy of Holies and never enter at all to look upon God?...we sense that the call is for us, but we still fail to draw near, and the years pass and we grow old and tired in the outer courts of the tabernacle. What hinders us?

A. W. Tozer, *The Pursuit of God*

In the Cleft of the Rock, 2013

Do I dare
ask God
for more of
Himself?

· · · · · ·

What hinders
me from
drawing near
and asking for
more of God?

· · · · · ·

Will I surrender
to the hand
of God, enter
the cleft of the
rock, and yield
to the unknown
to draw nearer
to the One I
love, the One
who loves?

Journey into Freedom

Have you ever played in your prayer? This image began as I sat with my girls and we created together. I had no plan as we began, just a desire to be attentive to God with my girls.

We created together, with God. My heart was prayerful as I chose colors I was drawn to and I allowed my hand to be free. Michaella hit the first bump in the road and angrily turned her paper over for a fresh start. As I had many times before, I encouraged her, "Don't give up." Hannah was doing alright, but she had chosen a challenging project. She set out to draw a self-portrait, and I saw her frustration as she struggled to translate the image from her mind to the paper. I coaxed and encouraged, "Don't give up...this may become your best work yet."

After mothering and affirming my daughters, I turned my attention to the paper before me. I assessed with a critical eye, and I saw chaos and a lack of design. Discouragement rose within me, and the condemning voice of perfectionism surfaced. I evaluated—it was no good. I felt small and inadequate.

But, God nudges, and eventually my mother-self takes center stage again. I must role model what I have been teaching. I watch Michaella furiously placing colors, lots of colors, and marks on her paper, and Hannah is diligent and focused, intently seeking to bring that which is real to the surface of the paper.

I toss the cloak of perfectionism aside, and I press on. I pick up my paintbrush and allow the colors to speak—this painting is about freedom. Freedom is the word that has been echoing in my soul for months now, freedom born out of love, not rebellion. True freedom rejects fear and embraces life in God.

Six days before the Passover, Jesus came to Bethany, where Lazarus lived, whom Jesus had raised from the dead. Here a dinner was given in Jesus' honor. Martha served, while Lazarus was among those reclining at the table with him. Then Mary took about a pint of pure nard, an expensive perfume; she poured it on Jesus' feet and wiped his feet with her hair. And the house was filled with the fragrance of the perfume.

John 12:1-3

For you were called to freedom...
Galatians 5:13 NASB

Surrender to anything other than love would be idiocy. Alarm bells should go off when we hear of people surrendering to abusive relationships. Surrender involves too much vulnerability to be a responsible action in relation to anything other than unconditional love. Ultimately of course this means that absolute surrender can only be offered to Perfect Love. Only God deserves absolute surrender, because only God can offer absolutely dependable love.

David Benner, *Surrender to Love*

Jesus said, "If you hold to my teaching, you are really my disciples.

Then you will know the truth, and the truth will set you free."

John 8:31b-32

Wings, 2012

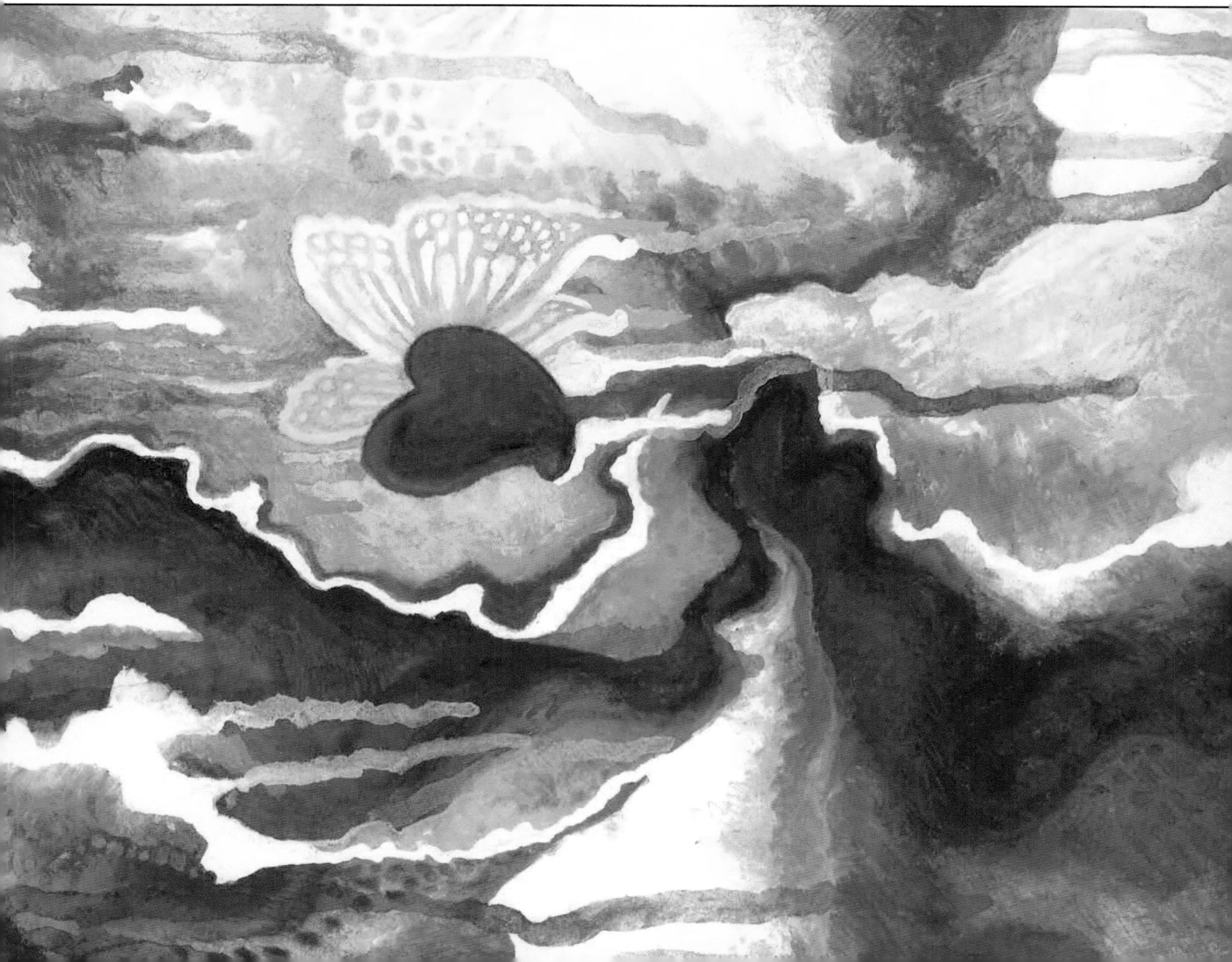

What hinders the freedom I have in God?

· · · · · ·

Where do I feel driven rather than drawn?

· · · · · ·

Where do I sense God's invitation to greater freedom?

His Workmanship

What do you do when your emotions are in a tangle? On this day I was tangled inside and conscious of my need of God. I wanted to let go of the layers of my independence and yield to God's Spirit. Surrender. So with pastels and paints I prayed on paper.

As a sacred practice I consciously adopted a posture that was open and undefended before God. I let go of my need to "hold it all together," and I leaned in to my Creator. I relinquished those things that seemed to bind me rather than deepen my freedom in Christ.

Big eyes, big brown eyes, appeared toward the center of the page as my prayer took form. My desire for understanding, for clarity, for discernment became part of the image as the swirling blues appeared. Free flowing earth tones reflected raw, earthy emotions. A bright yellow sphere spoke to me of light, God's light: choose Light.

God whispered to me of abiding, and a dark winding vine crept across the page. Jesus told His disciples at the Last Supper to abide in Him. The gift of the vine allures me. We were never intended to do life on our own but rather to be united to God through abiding in Jesus Christ. Living life in dependence leads to union that brings about transformation. And, finally, the butterfly emerges in the center of my paper.

The marks on the paper are raw and messy, but it feels authentic. I sense that I have been with God, and He has reached within my soul deeper than I can access alone.

What is my God-created essence? What does God see when He looks at me? Can I be free of the self I have created, my flesh? I choose to abide, for I long to be transformed by His hand.

Genuine transformation requires vulnerability. It is not the fact of being loved unconditionally that is life-changing. It is the risky experience of allowing myself to be loved unconditionally. Paradoxically, no one can change until they first accept themselves as they are. Self-deceptions and an absence of real vulnerability block any meaningful transformation. It is only when I accept who I am that I dare to show you that self in all its vulnerability and nakedness. Only then do I have the opportunity to receive your love in a manner that makes a genuine difference.

David Benner, *Surrender to Love*

For we are God's handiwork, created in Christ Jesus to do good works, which God prepared in advance for us to do.

Ephesians 2:10

Above all else, guard your heart, For everything you do flows from it.

Proverbs 4:23

"I am the true vine, and my Father is the gardener. He cuts off every branch in me that bears no fruit, while every branch that does bear fruit he prunes so that it will be even more fruitful. You are already clean because of the word I have spoken to you. Remain in me, as I also remain in you. No branch can bear fruit by itself; it must remain in the vine. Neither can you bear fruit unless you remain in me. I am the vine; you are the branches. If you remain in me and I in you, you will bear much fruit; apart from me you can do nothing."

John 15:1-5

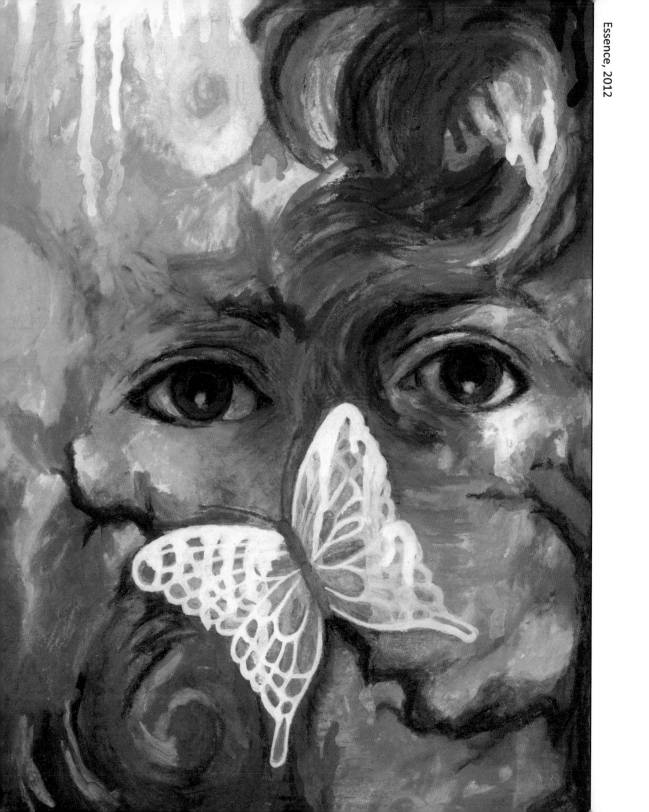

What
does true
freedom
look like
for me?

......

What does
God see
when He
looks at me?

His Workmanship

In All Things God Works

Have you ever found that truth sneaks up on you? I am convinced that sometimes God will surprise us, so it is best to be attentive. This drawing was done from a photograph I took at the home of my brother and sister-in-law. My intent was to capture the butterfly, and I did.

The photo of the Monarch was striking, but upon reflection I was drawn to the flowers in the image. Some of the flowers were brilliant and thriving; some were damaged but beautiful nonetheless. And some of the flowers were dead or dying.

I had been working on this drawing for a couple days when a thought stirred within me. The Scripture says that "in all things God works for the good of those who love Him." This would certainly encompass those things in our lives that are vibrant and alive. But it would also include those things that we would often discard: our brokenness, our failures, our weakness, and our dying. What a gift of grace that God will use all that is yielded to Him for our transformation. Will I entrust all to Him?

In All Things God Works

But whenever anyone turns to the Lord, the veil is taken away.

Now the Lord is the Spirit, and where the Spirit of the Lord is, there is freedom.

And we all, who with unveiled faces contemplate the Lord's glory, are being transformed into His image with ever-increasing glory, which comes from the Lord, who is the Spirit.

2 Corinthians 3:16-18

And we know that in all things God works for the good of those who love him,
who have been called according to his purpose.
For those God foreknew he also predestined to be conformed to the image of his Son,
that he might be the firstborn among many brothers and sisters.
And those he predestined, he also called; those he called,
he also justified; those he justified, he also glorified.

Romans 8:28-30

What do I see in my life as successes, victories, strengths, or even gifts?

••••••

What are those things that I see as failures, trials, weaknesses, or losses?

••••••

How might God use those things I consider failures or weaknesses as a canvas upon which He can display His grace and goodness?

Entrusting the Past

From the very beginning, when the first man and woman chose to act independently of God and with each subsequent act of our independence, we have felt the consequences of our sin and the sin of others. Our world is broken, and we are broken.

God has provided redemption and healing in His Son, Jesus, and one day that restoration will be complete. Jesus' death on the cross, His burial, and His resurrection reveal what God is doing now, in part, and what He will complete in the fullness of time. But for today, the invitation is to entrust to Him the brokenness within our lives. Some have endured great violence against their hearts, their souls, and their bodies. Some have experienced losses and betrayals so great that healing seems impossible.

We have encountered evil. And we have seen the hatred within us and outside of us—either malicious intent or self-righteous indifference. We have been unable to fix what is broken, and we have judged and condemned when it was not our right to do so.

This drawing is about entrusting the past to our Redeemer. He is the One who was present in the midst of the deepest darkness, and the One who journeys with us all the way to the place of full and complete healing: resurrection. Jesus experienced suffering at the cross in such a way that He knows our pain like no other. He understands.

God will judge evil, and God will heal. The cross offers us a place for healing, repentance, forgiveness, and release from the past.

There was a time I stood with someone I loved who had known great oppression and suffering. But my own brokenness hindered my response to the pain and compromised my ability to love. The Divine Healer asks us to entrust all that is broken to Him. The flower in this drawing speaks of healing.

As Jesus was on his way, the crowds almost crushed him. And a woman was there who had been subject to bleeding for twelve years, but no one could heal her. She came up behind him and touched the edge of his cloak, and immediately her bleeding stopped.

"Who touched me?" Jesus asked.

When they all denied it, Peter said, "Master, the people are crowding and pressing against you."

But Jesus said, "Someone touched me; I know that power has gone out from me."

Then the woman, seeing that she could not go unnoticed, came trembling and fell at his feet. In the presence of all the people, she told why she had touched him and how she had been instantly healed. Then he said to her, "Daughter, your faith has healed you. Go in peace."

Luke 8:42b-48

The Lord reigns forever;
he has established his throne for judgment.
He rules the world in righteousness
and judges the peoples with equity.

The Lord is a refuge for the oppressed,
a stronghold in times of trouble.
Those who know your name trust in you,
for you, Lord, have never forsaken those who seek you.

Psalm 9:7-10

God Heals, 2013

What is God asking me to entrust to Him?

······

Are there wounds from the past that only God can heal?

······

What would it take to reach out for healing?

On the day I called, You answered me;
You made me bold with strength in my soul.

Psalm 138:3 NASB

Embracing Flight

A New Way of Being

By design, the seasons repeat in the created world: winter, spring, summer, and fall. I expect that for most of us there will be more than one transformative season in our life's journey. As I look back in my life thus far I see three significant winter seasons of darkness—seasons where God was present, but life was painful and difficult, and sometimes God was silent. Each season of darkness entrusted to His hand ultimately was followed by spring—new life and growth—that resulted in fruitfulness. And each new learning built upon the last.

When a caterpillar egg hatches, a very hungry, tiny creature crawls into the world. This baby begins to eat—a lot. And then it starts to grow. As it grows its skin gets tight, and when that skin has outlived its usefulness, it is shed; this occurs 4 to 5 times before the caterpillar is full grown. Stages of growth and change, letting go to mature further.

God created living things with hunger. When the hunger is fed appropriately, things grow and mature as they were designed to. When we feed our hunger with those things God intended, we grow and mature as God intended. When we pay attention to the desire God placed within us for Himself, our soul matures.

One day the caterpillar will stop eating, anchor to a stable surface, and form a chrysalis. In that quiet, dark place, the caterpillar's structures and tissues are deconstructed and then reformed into the structures and tissues of a new creature. The metamorphosis usually takes a week or two although it is possible for the pupa, the caterpillar in the chrysalis, to enter a resting state for a few months or for the winter.

When it is time, the creature struggles forth, emerging from its encasement. This is a vulnerable stage in its life as it extends newly formed wings, pumping fluid into the veins of its wings. It stretches out in the sun, allowing the heat to harden its wings. A butterfly is a fully formed and mature creature, and now it is ready for flight. This creature will no longer function in this world the way it had before. It will move differently, eat differently, and see differently. It has been transformed.

When I awake in the morning I rarely remember my dreams. And if I do, they do not have a magical or adventurous quality to them, despite my childhood love of fantasy literature, complete with dragons, unicorns, and wizards. I suppose in many ways I am a realist, but this one night I had a dream that was magical. I could fly.

I'm not sure if I had feathers like a bird, or wings like a dragon, but somehow in my mind's eye I could soar above the earthbound. And not only could I fly, but I could see. My vision was not just clearer, but I could see differently. I don't remember if the colors were richer or the edges more precise, but I could see more than I had been able to see before. When I awoke I was intrigued by my unusual dream, and I wondered if there was a hint of something true within it. Things were shifting within me, and I was learning a new way of being.

A Focused Life

In early 2013 I approached the final months of spiritual direction training. The program had taught me the skills and the perspective that equipped me to listen and companion well, and on a personal level I had felt God's redemptive touch. I was not the same. The way I loved and the way I lived were different. I was less driven and more willing to relinquish the striving to get everything right. I still longed for righteousness. But I had given up trying to fix what was not mine to fix, and I was willing to let God be God. In my own life that simply involved receiving God's love, being myself, and walking with God. I was more confident in my calling and gifting—my life had become focused.

My life focus included this new work of spiritual direction and the renewal of my passion to create, but it also encompassed my roles as wife, mother, homemaker, and neighbor. It included the joy of a new vision for a drawing and the nitty gritty of pressing on with my drawing when the process became challenging. It included assuring my daughters of God's love and my love, as well as cleaning bathrooms, grocery shopping, helping with homework, and training my girls with life skills, such as keeping their rooms clean. Companioning a client and offering compassion to a neighbor were also part of my work. And all of it, from the mundane to the visionary, was to be offered to God, but even more so, to be lived with Him.

My passion was becoming more focused—it centered around our need to create space in our lives to listen for God. Listening is the beginning of communion with Him. Scripture tells us that our being, our living, our loving, and our serving is designed to flow out of our relationship with God. We were never intended to function independently but rather in union with God, through Jesus our Savior. A union not of equals, but of Creator and creature. God longs to be our source, our guide, and the love of our life.

As so many who had gone before me, in the pages of Scripture and in history, I had experienced my own inadequacy apart from God. Remember Moses, Peter, David, and Paul, to name just a few. What set these individuals apart? In the end, it was not their skills or their performance. Ultimately, each one allowed God's love to define them. They opened up to God's love, and God poured Himself in. God called them friends and entrusted His heart to them, then He moved through them to further His kingdom. We are not puppets controlled by strings but friends, chosen and appointed (John 15).

That spring was a season of discernment. I had heard God's invitation to partner with Him, to co-author my life, and to participate in His activity in the world. God affirmed my calling in startlingly clear and compassionate ways. Even as the moon lights the darkness, I was to light the darkness—reflecting the light of Jesus, God's Son, "the radiance of God's glory and the exact representation of His nature" (Hebrews 1:3, NASB). Dan Allender states in his book, *To Be Told*, "Our dreams must reflect the unimaginable—that we will reflect the character and glory of God into the lives of other people."

Invitation to Serve

Spiritual direction is an ancient practice, a ministry of listening and companionship. It is often pictured by three chairs because the third chair represents God, who is the true Director.

In February I met with my spiritual director, and I was anxious. Spiritual direction training would soon be complete, and I felt so uncertain. There were questions tumbling around in my soul. I rested in God's grace, I knew I was loved by God, and I had even experienced His affection and delight. But how did God see me as His partner, as one entrusted with His mission of love? I was trained and equipped but...? It was my heart's desire to companion others in their journey to experience God's love. Yet, I wavered.

My spiritual director welcomed me, and I sat on the couch across from him. In this space of prayer, he encouraged me to be still and attentive to my heart and the Spirit of God within. He struck the chime with a small wooden mallet, and as the tone echoed, the quiet settled around me.

As I sat in the silence, my thoughts turned to the weekend in Texas more than two years before when Pres encouraged me to ask God what He called me. God reminded me that He calls me "Beautiful." Now in the stillness I heard Him speak again: "Healer." My resistance was immediate. The words echoed four times: "Beautiful Healer." I struggled with doubt, and He said, "You are becoming what I intend." I had asked for God's affirmation, but I could feel the pull to disbelief. Why would God Almighty affirm me? The familiar insecurity surfaced.

I voiced my struggle, and my spiritual director asked, "What do you need? Ask for what you need." All that I needed was in God, I knew that. He was my strength and my source. As His emissary to His world, I needed to choose courage and belief. God had called me to partner with Him.

Shortly before dawn Jesus went out to them, walking on the lake. When the disciples saw him walking on the lake, they were terrified. "It's a ghost," they said, and cried out in fear.

But Jesus immediately said to them: "Take courage! It is I. Don't be afraid."

"Lord, if it's you," Peter replied, "tell me to come to you on the water."

"Come," he said.

Then Peter got down out of the boat, walked on the water and came toward Jesus. But when he saw the wind, he was afraid and, beginning to sink, cried out, "Lord, save me!"

Immediately Jesus reached out his hand and caught him. "You of little faith," he said, "why did you doubt?" And when they climbed into the boat, the wind died down.

Matthew 14:22-32

The scriptures are clear that discernment, when it is given, is always a gift. We cannot force discernment, but we can find ways to open ourselves to it. It is not accessed through a formula or a method; it is a way of being with a decision in God's presence and allowing him to guide our knowing. The capacity to discern and do the will of God arises out of friendship with God, cultivated through prayer, times of quiet listening and alert awareness.

Ruth Haley Barton, *Sacred Rhythms*

Be strong and let your heart take courage, All you who hope in the Lord.

Psalm 31:24 NASB

The Third Chair, 2013

How has God equipped me to partner with Him?

• • • • • •

What is my desire, and what is my hesitation?

• • • • • •

What do I need in order to partner with God as He is Light and Love in the world?

Journey of Discernment

Each weekend when I drove to the Jesuit Retreat Center, I would finally come to the wrought iron gate that marked the entrance to the property. Somehow that moment of arrival was always significant. There was a sense of peace that would settle upon me. I could feel myself let go of the stresses that had weighed me down, and my body would breathe a sigh of relief.

It was not that this place was magical. But it had been set aside for sacred purposes. And the individuals who attended were often consciously choosing to trust God or at least to engage in conversation with Him. God honors that intention of turning toward Him and seeking Him.

The gate was beautiful, standing tall and stately, as it marked the entrance to the Jesuit Center. I wanted to draw this structure, so one training weekend I walked down the long driveway to take photos. What a challenging venture—nothing seemed to lend itself to a drawing. I tried numerous angles, and nothing looked quite right. I was frustrated. But then, I paused and looked through the gate to see the road going up through the trees and the door of the gate which was swung open. The perspective had made all the difference. Click—I snapped the picture.

This drawing feels like an invitation, but what could the invitation be? Perhaps the ambiguity is meaningful in itself. This image reminds me that perspective can hinder or enhance our understanding.

A gate marks a boundary line. The gate may be open or closed—but there is a choice as you approach. Will you enter or not? Some gates are intended to keep danger out and to protect what is within. Some gates simply mark a property line, beyond which hospitality is offered. What does the gate mean to you?

The Lord is my shepherd, I lack nothing.
He makes me lie down in green pastures,
he leads me beside quiet waters, he refreshes my soul.

He guides me along the right paths for his name's sake.
Even though I walk through the darkest valley,
I will fear no evil, for you are with me;
your rod and your staff, they comfort me.

You prepare a table before me in the presence of my enemies.
You anoint my head with oil; my cup overflows.
Surely your goodness and love will follow me
all the days of my life, and I will dwell in the house of the Lord forever.

Psalm 23

Discernment is first of all a habit, a way of seeing that eventually permeates our whole life. It is the journey from spiritual blindness (not seeing God anywhere or seeing him only where we expect to see him) to spiritual sight (finding God everywhere especially where we least expect it).... The habit of discernment is a quality of attentiveness to God that is so intimate that over time we develop an intuitive sense of God's heart and purpose in any given moment.

Ruth Haley Barton,
Sacred Rhythms

This day I call the heavens and the earth as witnesses against you that I have set before you life and death, blessings and curses. Now choose life, so that you and your children may live and that you may love the Lord your God, listen to his voice, and hold fast to him. For the Lord is your life, and he will give you many years in the land he swore to give to your fathers, Abraham, Isaac and Jacob.

Deuteronomy 30:19-20

The Open Gate, 2012

Is there a gate before me?

• • • • • •

What will the choice to enter mean for me? What will the choice to avoid entrance mean for me?

• • • • • •

What perspective do I need in order to see the gate and the boundary line with clarity?

Trusting His Intention

What captivates you? In the spring of 2013, I was drawn to the beautiful description in Hosea 2 of God alluring Israel, His estranged beloved. The image of God drawing us to Himself, despite our adulterous hearts, moves me. And I am captivated by His tenderness.

The Hosea passage had been on my heart for a while, but somehow the months had slipped by before I attempted the drawing. I finally sat down with my colors and put my thoughts on paper. When a drawing is almost complete I will place it in a frame in my home so that I can live with it. This is a significant part of my process with God. My understanding of the Scripture passage, or the prayer, often deepens as I spend time with the drawing. I listen.

Initially when I encountered the Scripture, I was moved by God's allurement of the beloved. I had heard God's tender words myself and felt His invitation stir my desire for Him. But now I stood in a place of waiting. And I wondered at God leading His beloved into the wilderness. When I was first drawn to the passage, I had not noticed this space between the tender allurement and the door of hope. The space "between" is rarely easy.

As I sat with my drawing, I noticed how the lonely, wilting plant in the wilderness mirrored my own soul. And yet I knew the security of the tender words of God. So I waited. I could see the whole picture, and I knew the story. So, even though I understood that the next chapter might not look like I expected, hope strengthened my soul, for my God is trustworthy.

White in my drawings often reflects God or the Spirit of God. The white pigment carries this heart from the darkness into the allurement, through the wilderness and the valley of trouble, to the door of hope and into fruitfulness and intimacy.

"Therefore I am now going to allure her; I will lead her into the wilderness and speak tenderly to her.

There I will give her back her vineyards, and will make the Valley of Achor a door of hope.

There she will respond as in the days of her youth, as in the day she came up out of Egypt.

"In that day," declares the Lord, "you will call me 'my husband';

you will no longer call me 'my master.' I will remove the names of the Baals from her lips; no longer will their names be invoked."

Hosea 2:14-17

To really open myself to knowing and doing the will of God requires trust that God's intentions toward me are deeply good. Discernment requires interior freedom, a state of wide openness to God and the capacity to relinquish whatever might keep me from choosing for God. It is the belief held deep in the core of my being that God's will is the best thing that could happen to me under any circumstances.

Ruth Haley Barton, *Sacred Rhythms*

But you are a chosen people, a royal priesthood, a holy nation, God's special possession, that you may declare the praises of him who called you out of darkness into his wonderful light. Once you were not a people, but now you are the people of God; once you had not received mercy, but now you have received mercy.

1 Peter 2:9-10

I Will Allure Her, 2013

What has allured my heart, drawing me toward God's love and purpose for me?

• • • • • •

Has God led me into the wilderness?

• • • • • •

How has God drawn me into intimacy with Himself?

• • • • • •

Do I see the fruit of my relationship with Him?

Journey into Love

The sheltering tree's tangled limbs reach to the ground, and although it is large, it is easily overlooked. But if you wander close, duck beneath its limbs, and enter the tree, something changes and your heart may be touched. There is a sense of being protected and covered.

The beauty of this tree is not minimized by scarred trunk or gnarled branches, evidence of storms weathered and seasons endured. A strong core supports an abundance of foliage, providing a covering for all who walk beneath its canopy.

Perhaps this tree is a metaphor for a life that offers itself for another. Parents, friends, pastors, mentors, spiritual directors, teachers, and more—we offer our lives in love. God touches others through lives yielded to Him. The sheltering life is a shadow of the shelter provided by God. Follow the shadow, and you will find the real thing.

My friend teaches preschool, and she cares for little ones all day long, an exhausting job. But I have watched her with children. She truly enjoys them and loves them, and they know it. I have watched my daughters when they spend time with her, and they sparkle; they feel their own value by seeing her delight in them. It is not that she is all hugs, treats, and play, for I have watched her correct and teach my girls. But they know she likes them—not that she always likes how they behave, but she likes them.

Although my friend may have just a short time with the children entrusted to her care, they experience a taste of God's love. Perhaps one day when they feel God's love directly, they will more readily trust because of the love they experienced from one of His followers. And I expect that was His plan all along.

This is how God showed his love among us: He sent his one and only Son into the world that we might live through him. This is love: not that we loved God, but that he loved us and sent his Son as an atoning sacrifice for our sins. Dear friends, since God so loved us, we also ought to love one another. No one has ever seen God; but if we love one another, God lives in us and his love is made complete in us.

This is how we know that we live in him and he in us: He has given us of his Spirit. And we have seen and testify that the Father has sent his Son to be the Savior of the world. If anyone acknowledges that Jesus is the Son of God, God lives in them and they in God. And so we know and rely on the love God has for us.

God is love. Whoever lives in love lives in God, and God in them. This is how love is made complete among us so that we will have confidence on the day of judgment: In this world we are like Jesus. There is no fear in love. But perfect love drives out fear, because fear has to do with punishment. The one who fears is not made perfect in love.

We love because he first loved us.

1 John 4:9-19

The Sheltering Tree, 2011

What does
my life
offer to the
world?

• • • • • •

How am I
uniquely
created to
offer shelter
to another?

• • • • • •

How might
someone be
drawn more
deeply into
the heart
of God by
experiencing
my love and
care?

A New Way of Being

This butterfly is the same Monarch that my husband photographed in my hands. Now, after reading a bit about butterflies, I think this one may have been just out of its chrysalis, still stretching and drying its wings. Perhaps that is why it allowed me to hold it as we walked the block and a half to my house.

I had set it on the flowers in front of our home for this picture. It paused, perfectly still for a short while. And then, suddenly, it took off. It crossed the street, flew high above the houses, and then disappeared.

That caterpillar had traveled a long way to become something that it had not been before. It had begun as an insect that crawled along the ground, munching as it went, but now this transformed creature had a whole new way of being. It had been on a *journey to become*.

As I completed training for spiritual direction, I hesitated. I needed to hear God's affirmation, and yet I had heard it, distinctly. But the questions still echoed.

Self-doubt cloaked my soul. As I sat in class during one of our final training weekends, a friend described how self-sufficiency was familiar to her, yet God was calling her to dependence on Himself. I realized in that moment that my struggle was similar. Self-doubt was familiar, and I had wrapped this insecurity around my soul like a favorite old sweater. God was asking me to discard the persona I had adopted that identified with a sense of inadequacy; it was not my true self. Tears flowed down my cheeks at my hesitation to trust God's leading.

My supervisor asked me very directly what authority I was listening to—the voice of self-doubt is not the voice of God. My heart's desire was to follow God, and He was inviting me to flight...to confidence in Him. It felt awkward, but the adventure was enticing. Desire stirred within me to be brave, so I embraced all that He was leading me toward.

The butterfly hesitated as it stretched and dried its wings, the final stage of becoming. Finally, she took flight with new freedom.

But whenever anyone turns to the Lord, the veil is taken away. Now the Lord is the Spirit, and where the Spirit of the Lord is, there is freedom. And we all, who with unveiled faces contemplate the Lord's glory, are being transformed into his image with ever-increasing glory, which comes from the Lord, who is the Spirit.

2 Corinthians 3:16-18

Not that we are adequate in ourselves to consider anything as coming from ourselves, but our adequacy is from God.

2 Corinthians 3:5 NASB

A New Way

There are desires that are deep, true and fundamental to our being in Christ; these are the "desires of your heart" that God promises to fulfill (Psalm 37:4), although often differently from how we might have envisioned. A profound life orientation is revealed in these deepest desires, and when we come in touch with them, we have found God's direction for our life. This usually also has something to do with our calling, the purpose for which God created us. That is that part of ourselves—a passion or a burden that we carry that is uniquely ours—and it cannot be set aside lightly.

Ruth Haley Barton, *Sacred Rhythms*

Free to Fly, 2013

What familiar belief about myself have I wrapped up in like a favorite sweater? Is that belief what God says about me?

• • • • • •

Is God inviting me to a new way of being in the world?

• • • • • •

What would it take to discard that old sweater and allow God to wrap me up in Himself?

Metaphor

Therefore if anyone is in Christ, he is a new creature; the old things passed away; behold, new things have come.

2 Corinthians 5:17 NASB

This drawing tells a story of transformation. It begins with a hungry caterpillar whose life consists of crawling along branches and among the blades of grass. Then one day an internal prompt guides it to form a chrysalis, and it is enveloped for a time in silence and darkness. In that place all is hidden, and definition, of what was and what will be, disappears for a while.

But there comes a time when the creature that is being transformed hears the invitation to come forth. And with no great effort, the new being struggles to break out of its encasement. This butterfly pauses, held by protective hands, pumping fluid through its wings, and stretching them to dry. In the drawing this butterfly is white and what will be is not yet fully known.

Gradually, the creature's colors emerge as it moves into the Light. The butterfly takes flight. And finally those colors flow outward to touch others with God's love. The butterfly, transformed in the darkness by Love and Light, held by Love, united with Love, to offer Love.

Where are you in your story of transformation? What is the Designer and Author's invitation to you? How are you co-authoring your story with Him?

You, O LORD, keep my lamp burning; my God turns my darkness into light.
As for God his way is perfect; the word of the LORD is flawless.
He is a shield for all who take refuge in him.

For who is God besides the LORD? And who is the rock except our God?
It is God who arms me with perfect strength and makes my way perfect.
He makes my feet like the feet of a deer; he enables me to stand on the heights.

You give me your shield of victory and your right hand sustains me; you stoop down to make me great.
You broaden the path beneath me, so that my ankles do not turn.
The LORD lives! Praise be to my Rock! Exalted be God my Savior!

Psalm 18:16, 19, 28-36, 46 NIV 1984

Metaphor

We don't just have stories; we are a story. It is our responsibility to know our story so we can live it out more intentionally and boldly for the Great Story, the Gospel. God writes our story not just for our own enlightenment and insight, but to enlighten others and to reveal his own story through ours.

Dan Allender, *To Be Told*

To him who is able to keep you from stumbling and to present you
before his glorious presence without fault and with great joy—to the
only God our Savior be glory, majesty, power and authority, through
Jesus Christ our Lord, before all ages, now and forevermore! Amen.
Jude 1:24-25

Can I see God's hand in my story?

• • • • • •

Have I glimpsed the color of my wings?

• • • • • •

If things appear dark and the light is hidden now, can I grasp hold of hope and trust that God works in the darkness?

References

Longing for Something More

Journey to Become
Reprinted from *The Pursuit of God* by A.W. Tozer, copyright © 1948, 1982, 1993 by Zur Ltd. Used by permission of WingSpread Publishers, a division of Zur Ltd., 800.844.4571. p. 11

Held Secure
Taken from *The Gift of Being Yourself* by David G. Benner. Copyright ©2004 by David G. Benner. Used by permission of InterVarsity Press, PO Box 1400, Downers Grove, IL 60515. www.ivpress.com. p. 49.

Invitation to Rest
Taken from *Invitation to Solitude and Silence* by Ruth Haley Barton. Copyright © 2004 by Ruth Haley Barton. Used by permission of InterVarsity Press, PO Box 1400, Downers Grove, IL 60515. www.ivpress.com. p. 59.

Held in His Hands
Taken from *Invitation to Solitude and Silence* by Ruth Haley Barton. p. 30.

Paths Beyond the Mess
Taken from *Sacred Rhythms* by Ruth Haley Barton. Copyright © 2006 by Ruth Haley Barton. Used by permission of InterVarsity Press, PO Box 1400, Downers Grove, IL 60515. www.ivpress.com. p. 25.

Invitation to Repent
Taken from *The Gift of Being Yourself* by David G. Benner. p. 73.

The Darkness Deepens

Invitation to Wait
Taken from *Adventures in Prayer* by Catherine Marshall. Copyright © 1975 by Catherine Marshall. Chosen Books, Inc. p. 42.

Beyond the Walls
Republished with permission of The Crossroad Publishing Company, from *The Heart of the World* by Thomas Keating. Copyright © 1981, 1999, 2008 by St. Benedict's Monastery. Permission conveyed through Copyright Clearance Center, Inc, p. 83.

Taken from *The Gift of Being Yourself* by David G. Benner. p. 61.

Not My Way But Yours
Prince Caspian by CS Lewis ©CS Lewis PTe Ltd 1951. Extract used by permission. p. 138.

Treasures in the Darkness

Text
Taken from Preston Gillham's e-mail. www.prestongillham.com

Offering the Pain
Taken from *Invitation to Solitude and Silence* by Ruth Haley Barton. p. 30.

Beauty on the Journey
Taken from *To Be Told* by Dan Allender. Copyright © 2005 by Dan B. Allender. WaterBrook Press, a division of Random House Inc., New York. p. 51.

A Place to Listen
Reprinted from *The Pursuit of God* by A.W. Tozer, pp. 64, 71.

Journey of Grief
Image of the sun found in *A Grace Disguised: Expanded Edition* by Jerry Sittser. Copyright © 1995, 2004 by Gerald L. Sittser. pp. 41-42.

Vision on the Journey
Taken from *Adventures in Prayer* by Catherine Marshall. pp. 37-38.

What Are You Doing Here?
Taken from *Invitation to Solitude and Silence* by Ruth Haley Barton. p. 21.

Transformed Through Surrender

Surrender to His Hands
Taken from *Surrender to Love* by David G. Benner. Copyright © 2003 by David G. Benner. Used by permission of InterVarsity Press, PO Box 1400, Downers Grove, IL 60515. www. ivpress.com. p. 10.

A Bold Request
Reprinted from *The Pursuit of God* by A.W. Tozer. p. 43.

Journey into Freedom
Taken from *Surrender to Love* by David G. Benner. p. 59.

His Workmanship
Taken from *Surrender to Love* by David Benner. p. 76.

Embracing Flight

Text
Description of butterfly life cycle based on *Butterflies of North America* by Jeffrey Glassberg. Copyright © 2004 by Jeffrey Glassberg, Sterling Publishing Co., Inc., New York. pp. 14-21. Taken from *To Be Told* by Dan Allender. p. 119.

Invitation to Serve
Taken from *Sacred Rhythms* by Ruth Haley Barton. p. 116.

Journey of Discernment
Taken from *Sacred Rhythms* by Ruth Haley Barton. p. 111.

Journey into Love
Taken from *Sacred Rhythms* by Ruth Haley Barton. p. 97.

Trusting His Intention
Taken from *Sacred Rhythms* by Ruth Haley Barton. p.117.

A New Way of Being
Taken from *Sacred Rhythms* by Ruth Haley Barton. p.122.

Metaphor
Taken from *To Be Told* by Dan Allender. p. 52.

CREATING SPACE TO LISTEN

Artist
Christine Labrum

Prints available for purchase at www.creatingspacetolisten.com